HD 58 ECO

The Economics of Clusters

Studies of Policy Reform

Series Editors
François Bourguignon and Daniel Cohen

This series brings new and innovative policy research to the forefront of academic and policy debates.

It addresses the widest range of policies, from macroeconomics to welfare, public finance, trade, migration or environment. It hosts collaborative work under the auspices of Cepr, Cepremap and the Paris School of Economics.

The Economics of Clusters

Lessons from the French Experience

Gilles Duranton, Philippe Martin,
Thierry Mayer, and Florian Mayneris

OXFORD
UNIVERSITY PRESS

OXFORD
UNIVERSITY PRESS

Great Clarendon Street, Oxford OX2 6DP

Oxford University Press is a department of the University of Oxford.
It furthers the University's objective of excellence in research, scholarship,
and education by publishing worldwide in

Oxford New York

Auckland Cape Town Dar es Salaam Hong Kong Karachi
Kuala Lumpur Madrid Melbourne Mexico City Nairobi
New Delhi Shanghai Taipei Toronto

With offices in

Argentina Austria Brazil Chile Czech Republic France Greece
Guatemala Hungary Italy Japan Poland Portugal Singapore
South Korea Switzerland Thailand Turkey Ukraine Vietnam

Oxford is a registered trade mark of Oxford University Press
in the UK and in certain other countries

Published in the United States
by Oxford University Press Inc., New York

© CEPREMAP, 2010

The moral rights of the authors have been asserted
Database right Oxford University Press (maker)

First published 2010

British Library Cataloguing in Publication Data

Data available

Library of Congress Cataloging in Publication Data

Library of Congress Control Number: 2010936874

Typeset by SPI Publisher Services, Pondicherry, India
Printed in Great Britain
on acid-free paper by
MPG Books Group, Bodmin and King's Lynn

ISBN 978-0-19-959220-3

1 3 5 7 9 10 8 6 4 2

Acknowledgements

We thank Gordon Clark, Daniel Cohen, Pierre-Philippe Combes, Ed Glaeser, Henry Overman, Michael Pflüger, Frédéric Robert-Nicond, William Strange, and Matt Turner for very helpful comments on earlier versions of this book.

Contents

Contents

Contents

1

Introduction

This book is about an old phenomenon that has recently caught the imagination and excitement of policy makers. Clusters are indeed nothing new. Some of the clusters like the City of London or Sheffield and Thiers's specialization into cutlery have been going on for hundreds of years. At least since Alfred Marshall's (1890) *Principles*, the tendency for industries to cluster in some areas and the economic benefits that come with this type of concentration have fascinated economists and geographers alike. However, it is only quite recently that policy makers joined the wave and began to include clusters in the set of instruments they can use for their industrial or regional policy agenda.

1.1 The resurgence of clusters and cluster policies

There are several reasons for this new popularity of cluster policies. The first is probably related to Silicon Valley's iconic example. Following its success, clusters have come to be seen by many as the magical formula for regional development, innovation, and growth. European clusters may be less famous than the American ones, but several have developed on a similar model. The cluster of Cambridge (sometimes called SiliconFen) and the French cluster Minalogic in Grenoble are now well established in the fields of microelectronics and software, whereas the Biovalley (Strasbourg, Basle, and Freiburg), Stockholm, Munich, and Cambridge have become leading clusters in bio-technologies. Second, Porter's (1990) book on the competitive advantage of nations and his subsequent work have also been extremely influential and successful at promoting cluster policies.

Behind these two related impulses, we attribute the popularity of cluster initiatives to two deeper causes. First, 'traditional' industrial and regional policies have fallen into disrepute. To caricature the situation in many countries until the 1980s, there was a simple division of labour within the policy mix of countries. Industrial policy was in charge of boosting 'competitiveness', often by spurring the development of national champions. It was sometimes conflated with and complemented by science and technology policy. Regional policy, on the other hand, was concerned by equity consideration. For many years, the UK and France attempted to decentralize economic activity away from their main region of concentration, Greater London and Greater Paris, respectively. In Italy, there were sustained attempts at relocating economic activity from the prosperous North to the impoverished South. Canada has tried to foster the development of its poorer maritime provinces, etc.

During the 1980s and 1990s, both sets of policies, industrial and regional, started to be viewed as failures. Industrial policy was costly and failed to transform national champions into world champions. Regional policy, however sustained, was seemingly unsuccessful at reducing regional disparities. Traditional industrial and regional policies were both abandoned or reduced to a minimum by the turn of the century. This apparent debacle of traditional instruments left a policy void.

Second, and unlike traditional industrial and regional policies which are conducted only by the highest level of governments, cluster policies can be implemented by all levels of governments. Hence the 'market' for cluster policies is much larger than those for traditional regional and industrial policies. In the USA, where the federal government has traditionally been reluctant to conduct either industrial or regional policy, many sub-national jurisdictions have turned to cluster policy instead.

It should be clear however that cluster policies are not a modern reincarnation of traditional industrial and regional policies combined. There are two differences. First, unlike old-style regional policy, equity considerations are not officially the main concern of cluster policies. Quite the opposite, by actively pushing firms to cluster, this type of strategy could deprive poor regions of any chance to attract economic activities. Second, a cluster policy is more demanding in terms of information than traditional industrial policies are as it requires to

3

pick not only the 'right' industries but also the 'right' territories. It is interesting to note that one of the fathers of Silicon Valley, Frederick Terman, who was the vice-president of Stanford University, was unable to replicate this experiment in New Jersey a few years later when called upon by the Bell Laboratories (Leslie and Kargon 1996). There exists actually very few examples of public policies that were successful in promoting clusters.

We believe that bringing more economic analysis to the study of clusters is a worthwhile endeavour. Cluster building and cluster development are now widely viewed as key pillars of several public policies with diverse objectives ranging from local development to innovation and competitiveness. There are countless cluster initiatives and policy reports calling for cluster strategies. This movement in favour of cluster policies has impacted many European countries and regions in the last thirty years. For instance, the European Cluster Observatory provides detailed reports about cluster initiatives in more than thirty European countries.[1] The Spanish Basque country was a pioneer in that matter. At the end of the 1980s, the economic situation of the Spanish Basque country was very bleak, with old industries and a high level of unemployment above the Spanish average. In that context, the Basque government asked Michael Porter to make a territorial diagnosis in order to redefine the economic strategy of the region. At the beginning of the 1990s, a few 'priority' clusters were identified, some

[1] See http://www.clusterobservatory.eu/.

of them in traditional industries (machine tools, harbour activities, etc.) and some others in more leading-edge industries (aeronautics, ICT, etc.), on which local authorities concentrated on R&D projects, cooperative training programmes, etc. The Basque region improved its performance with respect to other Spanish regions in terms of employment and wealth. The Basque unemployment rate became significantly lower than the Spanish one in the second half of the 1990s. This success has been attributed to the cluster strategy, and the example of the Spanish Basque country is often cited by European advocates of cluster policies. The German federal government chose in 1999 a strategy more directly based on information-sharing. It created a label, the 'Kompetenznetze' (networks of competence), for the 'best' German clusters. The label allows members to benefit from advertising through the website http://www.kompetenznetze. de and from actions aimed at promoting relations between firms, scientists, and investors within and across industrial fields. In France, the Local Productive Systems policy, implemented at the end of the 1990s, attempted to favour collaborative projects between firms from the same industry and located in the same area; we present this policy in more detail in Chapter 5. Finally, in 2006 and 2008, the European Commission published two papers[2] in which it encouraged member states to integrate cluster strategies in their national innovation

---

[2] *Putting Knowledge into Practice: A Broad-Based Innovation Strategy for the EU*, COM(2006) 502 and *Towards World-Class Clusters in the European Union: Implementing the Broad-Based Innovation Strategy*, COM(2008) 652.

programmes. The Commission also commits to provide assistance to countries in terms of experience-sharing. Moreover, several instruments of the European Union aimed at financing innovation and regional policy are dedicated to clusters. These actions, sometimes very different in their contents and their scale, have in the end a non-negligible financial cost. This is the case for example of, *inter alia*, the French 'competitiveness clusters', a policy implemented for three years starting in 2005 and extended to 2009–11 (1.5 billion euros for each phase), the 'BioRegio' programme (75 million euros from 1995 to 2005), and the 'Innovative Regional Growth Cores' programme (150 million euros since 2001) in Germany or the 'Production Industries in London' initiative (15 million euros for 2006–8) and the 'Northwest regional economic Strategy' (45 billion euros in 2006–9) in the UK.

1.2 Not much existing analysis

The analysis on clusters falls into one of three groups. First there are many 'policy' papers and reports on the subject. Among many, see for instance Department of the Environment, Transport, and the Regions (2000), Council on Competitiveness et al. (2001), Department of Trade and Industry (2001a), OECD (2001), European Commission (2003), Sölvell et al. (2003), Cortright (2006), and the many references therein. It is also possible to look at the papers of the recent TCI annual global conferences at http://www.competitiveness.org/.

This strand of literature is generally very favourable to cluster initiatives. As economists, our judgement on this literature is quite critical because proponents of cluster policies rarely call for a quantitative evaluation of the costs and benefits of these policies. The evaluation, when it exists, is usually a 'qualitative' and mostly descriptive exercise.

The second type of work on clusters is often done by geographers and sociologists. Their work is very useful to sharpen our understanding of how clusters work and what happens inside them. The path-breaking work on Italian 'industrial districts' edited in Pyke et al. (1990) provided numerous insights and a wealth of empirical evidence raising the awareness about clusters. This work has now developed into a large literature that has looked at hundreds of clusters (or closely related objects that are designated by different names) empirically and theorized on a variety of issues related to the benefits from clustering.

A complete review of this literature does not belong here. Interested readers could refer to, *inter alia*, Storper (1997), Maskell (2001), or Martin and Sunley (2003), for broad introductions. Here, it is enough to highlight that this literature mainly complements our work. A lot of the focus of geographers is on the detailed examination of the workings of clusters. The classic work of Saxenian (1994) on Silicon Valley is only the tip of a large series of case studies of clusters. One could also cite excellent work by Henry and Pinch on the British Motor Valley in a series of articles (see, for instance, Henry and Pinch

2000), etc. Related theoretical work is then used to theorize more broadly about the origins of the benefits from clustering. There is a strong emphasis on the benefits of proximity for the generation of new knowledge (Cooke 2001) and its circulation (Bathelt et al. 2004). To some extent, and along with the corresponding literature on those issues in economics (Duranton and Puga 2004), we use it as a foundation for some relationships within clusters that we do not fully explore.

Geographers also produced important insights for policy. Much of the cluster literature in geography rightly emphasizes two aspects. First, there seems to be a lot of heterogeneity, even among well-functioning clusters. Although this focus on the 'specific', as opposed to more general features of clusters, is sometimes viewed as a professional bias of geographers, it usefully cautions us about broad, one-size-fits-all policy proposals. Second, the benefits of clusters appear to rely on very subtle relationships that can take a broad variety of forms (Markusen 1996; Gordon and McCann 2000). Sometimes, they rely on competitive market interactions. At other times, they rely on non-market interactions, be they strong personal links or specific local institutions. These subtle advantages of existing clusters seem hard to replicate by policy. We return to this discussion below.

Despite these important insights, the geography literature is of limited interest for our purpose here. First, its focus is mostly on the benefits from concentration, which are often explored in great detail, whereas many of the costs of concentration and the imperfect mobility of factors are simply not part of the analysis. Put differently, the approach of geographers is too 'partial equilibrium' whereas we need a more 'general equilibrium' focus (though Storper 1997 is an exception). Second, geographers do not usually quantify their findings and have a tendency to shy away from policy discussions (Markusen 2003). The purpose of our work is instead to provide policy-relevant quantifications of the costs and benefits of clusters.

Finally, economists have showed some renewed interests in issues surrounding the location of economic activity. This new impetus can be traced back to Krugman (1991) on the theory side and Glaeser et al. (1992) on the empirical side. The economic analysis of cities and clusters is mostly concerned with assessing the benefits of concentration of economic activity and clustering as they happen in the 'real world'. Even though this literature on the evaluation of agglomeration economies has interesting implications for economic policy, it does not offer to date an evaluation of cluster initiatives. What this body of work actually does is to broadly confirm the starting point of cluster policies: clustering brings economic gains. In particular, firms' performance improves when they are located close to other firms in the same sector. However, these gains are modest. Our analysis of the French case confirms both the existence of gains from clustering and the fact that they are quantitatively modest. Importantly, the fact that gains from clustering exist is a necessary but not a sufficient condition to justify public intervention. Public intervention requires that the market equilibrium is suboptimal, for example because the location choice of firms leads to too little clustering. It is also necessary that public policies can generate either larger or better clusters. Our analysis of the French case suggests that these two conditions are difficult to meet.

1.3 Why France is interesting

Our empirical work focuses on the French case. We believe France is interesting for several reasons. First, there is a long tradition of strong government intervention regarding the location of economic activity. Until quite recently, the equity objective had long been dominant with the aim to spread economic activities over the whole territory and counter the dominance of Paris. However, following other initiatives in Europe and elsewhere, the French government first implemented its policy of the 'Local Productive Systems' (LPS), before developing an even more ambitious cluster initiative in 2005: the 'Pôles de Compétitivité' or competitiveness clusters. With these policies, the location of economic activity should now serve competitiveness and public policies should help to draw this efficient geography. These clusters are seen as a key element of a 'new industrial policy', to take the official term. It also reveals clearly that cluster policies in France and in the EU are often thought of as a way to circumvent the constraints on industrial policies and the fact that direct subsidies are forbidden by EU rules. In this case, economic geography is not only supposed to serve competitiveness but also the role of the state in the economy.

The change in public policy brought by this cluster initiative should not be underestimated. It comes after fifty years during which the main objective was to avoid growing economic disparities between regions and help regions in decline. The public discourse on economic geography used to presume that it could only be too concentrated and unequal. Today's public discourse is more balanced with a focus on potential economic gains from clusters: specialization, cooperation, and agglomeration of economic activities on the most dynamic territories should be encouraged by public policies. For a given sector and territory, a 'critical mass' must be attained to sustain international competition and the logic is clearly one of spatial concentration. Similarly, the spatial agglomeration is often presented as necessary to foster better collaborations and interactions between economic actors and help innovation.

However, spatial equity considerations have not disappeared in France: seventy-one competitiveness clusters exist today. They are strikingly well spread over the whole French territory. Although all clusters do not benefit from R&D subsidies, they all receive some sort of financial support, which reveals a particular attention from national policy makers to the fact that no region should feel neglected. These clusters are not the first cluster policy in France. Another public policy, called 'Système Productifs Locaux' for 'Local Production Systems' (LPS will be the acronym we use), was initiated in 1999 with similar objectives, although with a much smaller budget (the competitiveness clusters benefited from a budget of 1.5 billion euros over 2006–8 plus 1.5 billion euros for 2009–11). As in the case of the competitiveness clusters, the map of the LPS seems too egalitarian to be the outcome of its original objectives. Hence, it is clear that equity considerations have not disappeared from cluster policies. The contradictions and hesitations on economic geography are clearly still present and the coherence between the objectives and the implementation are not fully transparent.

The trade-off between equity and efficiency that may arise with regional policies is not specific to France but also arises in other large countries and in discussions on regional policies at the European level. Starting in the 1980s, there was a large increase in funds for regional policies and an explicit mention of the objective of reducing regional disparities in the Single European Act (Article 1). The European Union has been devoting an increasing share of its budget to regional policies. The Structural Funds and the Cohesion Fund represent around one-third of the 2004 Community budget. Some of these regional policies are based on ideas that are close to national cluster policies. In particular, the importance of local cooperation between actors (firms, local governments, universities, etc.) and of local spillovers is often stressed. Hence a better understanding of the mechanisms on which these policies are justified is important not only for the French case but also for policies at the European level and in other countries. The financial crisis has also led several European governments to rethink their industrial policies. For example, in the UK, Peter Mandelson's active industrialism is being interpreted as implying more clusters.[3] Finally, even though we do not believe that our results can extend to developing countries, some of the issues, theoretical questions, and empirical methodologies analysed in this book can be used for these countries. Given that agglomeration and spatial specialization have certainly not attained their steady state, these issues may actually be more important in developing countries. The story of Dongguan in China is certainly best described as one of a successful cluster story that exemplifies the economic gains of agglomeration. The World Development Report (World Bank 2009) entitled *Reshaping Economic Geography* shows that there is a strong policy interest in these issues in developing countries.

Another reason to study the French experience is that French cluster initiatives are unified across France. Although the sectors and the amount of subsidy vary, the general framework is the same everywhere and the same instruments are used. Hence clusters can be compared in cross-section rather than viewed as different and specific cases.

[3] Secretary of State for Trade and Industry in Tony Blair's government.

1.4 A summary of what comes next

Chapter 2 examines the economic mechanisms behind the clustering of economic activity. We agree with standard economic theory that local increasing returns are the core justification of the existence of clusters. With increasing returns at play, we do not expect the economy to reach full efficiency in the absence of intervention.

The fact that market forces do not produce an optimal distribution of economic activity across cities can justify public intervention. However, because of the large number and of the complexity of market failures that can act in opposite directions on the spatial concentration of economic activities, what public policies should do and how they should do it in this respect is not obvious. It is not immediately clear indeed whether there is too much or too little spatial concentration of economic activities, too much or too little specialization of territories. Cluster polices can also have negative effects when taking into account the political economy of decision making. Another issue is that a greater specialization of regions may be dangerous as specialized regions become very dependent on sectoral shocks. This problem is especially acute in Europe where labour mobility, even inside countries, is low compared for example to the US.

Chapter 3 contains some descriptive evidence about the concentration of sectors of economic activity in France and some measures of performance for those sectors. The lessons from this description of French economic geography are unclear in terms of policy re-commendations: over the past twenty years, we detect no clear link between the evolution of spatial concentration in France and the performance of industrial sectors. This lack of evidence could come from various composition effects, pointing to the need of deeper econometric analysis that study the effects of spatial concentration at the firm level.

In Chapter 4, we show that at the firm level, agglomeration economies do exist; but we also show that they are partly internalized by French firms in their location choices and that a considerable change of French geography would be necessary to make important productivity gains thanks to agglomeration economies.

More specifically, we first discuss the empirical literature on agglomeration effects. It shows that benefits from clusters do exist, in particular on local productivity. This evidence is now relatively well established. Using a very detailed firm-level data set, we confirm that the same type of result applies for France. We find that on average, doubling the number of employees of a given sector and a given territory increases the productivity of firms in this sector and territory by less than 5 per cent.

For the policy maker, the relevant question therefore becomes: to obtain an average productivity gain of around 5 per cent, can and should one aim to double the size of existing clusters and increase spatial concentration and specialization accordingly? Such a radical change in the distribution of economic activity in France looks beyond the scope of cluster policies. Hence, the logical conclusion is that the gains to be expected from a cluster policy are rather modest: no economic miracle there. Since our results are similar to those for other countries, this conclusion is not specific to the French case. The enthusiastic message of the proponents of cluster policies must be revised downwards.

Also, we find that the benefits of clustering are not uniform across sectors. Some sectors see their productivity increase when clustering but others (a minority though) seem to experience a productivity loss. An interesting finding is that there is no obvious classification of sectors that gain more from clustering. The exciting high-tech sectors that are at the core of many cluster policies do not seem to be different from other sectors. Likewise, there is no general tendency, in France, for all sectors to cluster over time. Some do and create 'natural' clusters but others tend to disperse, maybe to take advantage of lower wages or real estate prices in 'empty' regions. This also suggests that a uniform cluster policy or even a cluster policy aimed at the high-tech sectors may be dangerous. At a more fundamental level, our scepticism towards cluster policies originates from the simple fact that the local composition of economic activity is an intermediate outcome, not a fundamental driver of prosperity. Hence, cluster strategies must overcome two major difficulties. First, clustering is not a choice variable that local policy makers can easily manipulate. Second, this intermediate outcome is only weakly related to the final prosperity objectives that local policy makers should be interested in.

Our disagreement with cluster proponents does not mean that we want to revert to old-style regional policies aimed at dispersing economic activity. The benefits from concentration imply that forced dispersion is not efficient.

Finally, in Chapter 5, we study the first French cluster policy, the Local Productive Systems, and we show that beyond efficiency objectives, equity considerations were present in the implementation of that policy. Our analysis is based on a very rich French firm-level data set that allows us to evaluate the impact of the policy. To our knowledge this is the first evaluation of a cluster policy using firm-level data on a very large panel. We are able to evaluate the effect of the LPS policy on the total factor productivity of French firms. We first find that firms that entered an LPS produce in regions which are less productive than the average. Those firms are also on a bad trend in the sense that they belong to sectors which are not among the most dynamic ones and that their productivity is stagnating relative to other firms in the same sector and the same region. A selection effect is arguably present: the firms targeted by the cluster policy can be characterized, relative to the others, as losers. Clearly, strong political economy mechanisms were at work here. The traditional objectives of regional policy seem key to understanding the implementation of the policy even though the stated objectives were the opposite.

When comparing the productivity of firms before and after being 'treated' by the LPS policy, we find no difference. Nor do we find any impact on the attractiveness of the LPS territory as we find no difference in employment or in the number of firms in territories selected to be LPS. The public policy has not generated any clustering and this may be the reason why it has had no visible effect on the productivity of firms.

Not all our results are negative though: we find that single-plant firms benefit—in terms of productivity—from being part of an LPS. The gains are small (around 3 per cent) and more importantly disappear rapidly after two years. However, to be fair this policy was quite modest and not very costly to public finances. Also, it is impossible to say whether in the absence of such a cluster policy LPS firms would have experienced the same productivity stagnation or a strong fall in productivity. In the former case, we can be confident that there was no effect of the public policy. In the latter, more contrived case, the public policy has a positive effect. However, the LPS seemed to have targeted the firms in relative decline and from this point of view seem more defensive than offensive. We cannot firmly conclude from these results that cluster policies cannot have positive effects, but at least they should be seen as a warning that no miracle can be expected from cluster policies. Our conclusion is that if economic gains from clusters exist—and our results do point to such gains—but that existing cluster policies do not seem successful either in their intermediate goals (increasing the size of clusters) or their ultimate goals (increasing firms' productivity), then it may be time to think about alternative public policies in favour of clusters. Rather than centralized schemes where the state gives subsidies, we believe that one should focus on the brakes that impede the growth of the 'natural' clusters. Those impediments are linked to the mobility of factors, both workers and firms, or to regulations on housing.

2

The Economic Rationale of Clusters and Cluster Policies

2.1 A very simple model of clusters

2.1.1 Clusters in the policy literature: what is the rationale?

As noted above, the 'policy' literature on clusters is extensive. A comprehensive critical analysis is beyond the scope of this study. Instead, it is best to focus on the summary piece 'Location, competition, and economic development: local clusters in a global economy' by Michael Porter, the leading exponent of cluster strategies (Porter 2000b).[1]

---

[1] Other writings from the same author on the same topic (Porter 1998b, 2000a, 2003) contain the same definition for cluster and the same framework of analysis. Altogether the four aforementioned pieces have been cited nearly 1,500 times in the International Citation Index as of September 2010. Despite the short time span, this count demonstrates how influential these policy recommendations have been in academic circles. As for Porter's seminal book from 1990, the citation count nears 4,000 making it one of the most cited works in the last thirty years.

The oft-alleged problem with the policy literature on clusters is one of definition(s). This literature provides many definitions of what is a cluster. As noted by Martin and Sunley (2003), these definitions differ and are all rather vague. This multiplicity is certainly not helpful to the analyst trying to assess the concept. Focusing on Porter, his own definition is:

A cluster is a geographically proximate group of interconnected companies and associated institutions in a particular field, linked by commonalities and complementarities. (Porter 2000b: 16)

Following this definition a cluster, at a conceptual level, appears to be no more than the spatial agglomeration of a given 'activity' (or a 'field' using Porter's words). Although it is not clear what 'commonalities' and 'complementarities' are, this definition points at some benefits from agglomeration. Interestingly, Porter's definition is not very different from that used by mainstream regional and urban economists since Alfred Marshall (1890). For instance, Belleflamme et al. (2000: 161) define a cluster as a 'full or partial agglomeration in one region of firms...that benefit from each other's presence'. Within a theoretical model, this type of definition can be made precise. We show this below. Thus, *at a conceptual level*, the problem with the cluster literature may not be one of definition.[2] Instead, the problem

[2] Empirically, Porter's definition (just like that of Belleflamme et al. 2000) is of course more problematic since it is not obvious what an 'activity' is (in particular whether we can identify activities with 'sectors' as defined by

with the cluster policy literature is one of lack of well-articulated theory: what is the 'problem' that cluster initiatives are trying to fix?

A common response in the policy literature (Sölvell et al. 2003) is to argue that cluster initiatives are meant to improve local 'competitiveness'.[3] But a lack of competitiveness is a symptom, not the root of a problem. Put differently, improving an outcome such as competitiveness cannot be a sufficient justification for a policy. Instead, the goal of public policy should be to maximize social welfare by correcting existing inefficiencies (and inequities). To understand this difference, consider the following simple example. Faster technological progress is a desirable outcome. If firms invest efficiently, the best policy is to do nothing: public investment will crowd out private investment and incentives for firms to invest more will lead to a waste of resources. If firms invest inefficiently, it is fundamental to know why. If firms do not invest enough because their innovations get quickly imitated, the appropriate policy is to increase the protection of innovations. If instead the absence of investment is caused by credit constraints, policy should deal with this inefficiency. More generally, any policy proposal should

standard industrial classifications) and what geographical scale is involved in clustering. The discussion of these issues is postponed to section 4.1.

[3] While economic geographers like Martin and Sunley (2003) have a problem with the definition of clusters, economists usually take issues with the use of the word 'competitiveness'. As indicated by the writings of Porter, competitiveness seems to be synonymous with both productivity and productivity growth. It could also be read as productivity relative to competition. In most of what follows, competitiveness will be taken to mean productivity in levels. Productivity growth is discussed in section 2.2.

clearly identify some inefficiencies (or inequities) and explain how it will correct them.

To be fair, Porter in his writings is usually more concerned with articulating a rationale for his policies than most of his followers. The main theoretical tool used in Porter (2000b: 16) and in many of his other works is the 'competitive diamond' which purports to explain the 'sources of locational competitive advantage' (see Figure 2.1). The central part of this diamond is a dynamic 'local context' infused with 'vigourous competition'. This central element then feeds into four boxes:

Figure 2.1 Porter's competitive diamond
Source: Porter (2000b: 20).

'Firm Rivalry', 'Demand Conditions', 'Supporting Industries', and 'Input Conditions'. These four boxes are pairwise linked through two-way arrows. The interactions between the different components of the diamond are then alleged to generate the 'competitive advantage' of the cluster.

According to Porter, the role of (local) governments in this framework is to foster every single part of the diamond and strengthen the arrows that join them. Because the interactions between the parts of the diamond reinforce each other, an improvement in one box gets magnified through its interactions with the other components of the diamond. A number of policies are then attached to each part of the diamond. Porter (2000b) distinguishes between policies that make a cluster expand (such as 'efforts to attract suppliers and service providers from other locations' and various other subsidies to increase the employment size of the cluster) and policies that make clusters more competitive (e.g. 'creation of specialised education programmes', 'enhancement of specialised transportation', having local authorities 'acting as sophisticated buyer of the cluster's products', and a long list of other policies). Thus the final recommendation consists of many policies, all aimed at 'upgrading the cluster'. In turn, these interventions are alleged to result in a bigger and more competitive cluster.

The bottom line of Porter's framework is that clusters generate 'competitiveness' so that strengthening and developing clusters is a worthy policy objective. In turn, this requires a complex policy mix that is specific to each cluster.

From an economic policy perspective, there are three problems with Porter's framework. First, it is unnecessarily complicated. However, this complexity of the web of boxes and arrows of Figure 2.1 is only superficial because all the elements of the model are positively feeding into each other. Consequently, the improvement of any component of the model is going to be a good thing (though it is best to coordinate improvements so that they magnify each other). There is no suggestion that a negative feedback somewhere might make things more complicated.

Second, the complexity of Porter's framework masks the absence of crucial elements. That is, Porter's model of clusters is not fully specified. Then, nothing guarantees that the conclusions are warranted. For instance, nothing is said in Porter's framework about the mobility of labour. But, in the absence of assumptions about labour supply, how do we know that it makes sense to attract firms from outside the cluster? If labour is sufficiently immobile, this type of policy may entail considerable deadweight losses. To take another example, there is no explicit land market in Porter's framework. But then, how do we know that the surplus generated by a cluster (if any) is not going to benefit solely passive landowners? Even worse, incompletely specified models may contain hidden contradictions. For instance, the production structure in clusters and the way firms compete are not spelled out in Porter's framework. Then, it is unclear whether the removal of barriers to entry is consistent with an increased emphasis on new product development (both advocated by Porter (2000b: 28)). Often, these two recommendations are mutually inconsistent.[4] More generally, nothing guarantees that the conclusions of a model make any sense unless all the key relationships are made explicit and all the quantities are followed throughout the derivation of the key results.[5]

Third, the framework used by Porter and his followers does not really make the case for the local public policies they advocate. In a firm, if the management does nothing, chances are that nothing will happen. However, the benchmark for public policy is different. Public policy usually deals with situations in which independent economic agents make their own decisions, unlike passive employees who are waiting to be instructed by management. Any public policy proposal thus needs to show that it will improve on what happens in its absence. Put differently, the case needs to be made of an inefficiency (or several) that the policy will counter. This case simply is not made in Porter's analysis.[6]

---

[4] For firms to invest in new product development, they need to be able to appropriate some rents *ex post*. Removing barriers to entry is likely to reduce these rents and thus the *ex ante* incentive to invest.

[5] Being fully articulated does not require large numbers of variables in a model. Rather it is about making clear what the key simplifications made by the model are.

[6] To be fair, many of his policy recommendations such as creating training programmes or the elimination of local barriers to entry can easily be rationalized within a consistent framework. But then the proper justifications for these policies may not bear much relationship to clusters...

2.1.2 *Modelling clusters*

Economic theories concerned with cities, regions, or clusters have a common underlying structure.[7] This underlying structure contains three elements: a spatial structure, a production structure, and some assumptions about the mobility of goods and factors. These elements are necessary for any model to be well specified.

Spatial structure. Since clusters happen somewhere, some description of geography is obviously needed. It is often convenient to divide space into a number of areas and distinguish between the internal geography of these areas and their external geography. Internal geography is concerned with land, housing, infrastructure, and internal transport. External geography is about how areas are located relative to each other, the location of natural resources, the development of new areas, etc. Depending on the focus of the analysis, some aspects need to be spelled out in great detail while others can be modelled in a very simple fashion. For instance, models of cities often concentrate on their internal geography (land and commuting costs) and assume a very simple external geography. On the contrary, regional models usually propose a detailed modelling of the external geography of much larger areas, regions, but ignore the micro issues related to the operation of land markets. What about clusters then? Following the cluster policy literature, it is

---

[7] The material in this subsection borrows from Combes et al. (2005). Their basic framework has been adapted to the specific case of clusters as inspired by the classic work of Henderson (1974).

always possible to define spatial units that can be called 'clusters'.[8] Since the relative location of clusters and relative locations within clusters are not prominent concerns in that literature, we can ignore these issues and make the simplest possible assumptions about the internal and external geography of clusters. More specifically, we can think of clusters as areas that trade freely with each other and are endowed with symmetric sites.

Arguably a land market has to be explicitly introduced given the differences in land values across places and the importance of land development issues in local public policies. Hence the simplest model of clusters can assume that each cluster is an area endowed with a given amount of land.[9]

These extreme simplifications may seem unappealing. It should be kept in mind however that the objective here is to present the best case in favour of cluster policies. In other words, the starting point of the analysis made here is purposefully very close to that of cluster proponents. As it will turn out, this starting point makes sense empirically. The main problem with cluster proponents is not their starting point but the fact that

[8] As pointed out by Martin and Sunley (2003), this definition is somewhat tautological and may remind us of *Alice Through the Looking-Glass*'s Humpty Dumpty whose words meant what he chose them to mean, 'neither more nor less'. However this issue does not matter for the time being. The empirical content of this spatial zoning is postponed to section 4.1.

[9] A more sophisticated modelling of the internal and external geography of clusters may be desirable. The very simple assumptions made here are in the spirit of the policy literature and are enough to exhibit some key inefficiencies associated with clusters in absence of corrective policies (as well as show the ambiguities of cluster initiatives).

they do not rigorously follow through their policy argument and do not pay enough attention to the relevant magnitudes.

Production structure. It may be tempting to specify an aggregate production function that directly relates primary factors to the final output, as is customary in much of economic analysis. In the case of clusters, this standard simplification is not adequate. First, both the descriptive accounts of clusters (Porter 1990; Saxenian 1994) and the policy literature put a lot of emphasis on the roles of intermediate inputs, the local labour force, and non-market interactions. Second, clustering is often justified by appealing to some form of increasing returns. Understanding the inefficiencies associated with increasing returns calls for a detailed modelling of how they arise through the production process.

Three main mechanisms can be used to justify the existence of local increasing returns (Duranton and Puga 2004). First, a larger market allows for a more efficient *sharing* of indivisible facilities (e.g. local infrastructure), risks, and the gains from variety and specialization. For instance, a larger cluster in a given activity will make it easier to construct some dedicated facility or, for specialized input providers, to pay a fixed cost and enter the (larger) local market. Second, a larger market also allows for a better *matching* between employers and employees, buyers and suppliers, partners in joint projects, or entrepreneurs and financiers. This can occur through both a better quality of matches between economic agents and a higher probability of finding a match. Finally, a larger market can also facilitate *learning* about new technologies, market evolutions, or new forms of organization. More frequent direct interactions between economic agents in a cluster can thus favour the creation, diffusion, and accumulation of knowledge.[10]

There is a large theoretical literature that investigates the microeconomic foundations of local increasing returns in great detail (Duranton and Puga 2004). Two main conclusions can be drawn from that literature. First, local efficiency (in broad sense) is expected to increase with the local size of an activity. This is consistent with the implicit assumption made by most cluster proponents that bigger and more specialized is better. Second, the sources of local increasing returns are also sources of local inefficiencies. For instance, specialist input producers in a model with input–output linkages may not be remunerated for increasing the local choice of inputs. In a matching framework, firms are not compensated for increasing the liquidity of their local labour market. With local learning spillovers workers are not rewarded for the knowledge they diffuse. More generally,

[10] This typology differs from the traditional Marshallian 'trinity' (Marshall 1890), which talks of spillovers, input–output linkages, and labour pooling. In fact the two typologies complement each other. Marshall's is about 'where' those effects take place (market for labour, market for intermediates, and a mostly absent market for ideas) whereas the one used here is about the type of mechanism at stake (sharing, matching, learning). Arguably, these three mechanisms (and their associated market failures) can take place in different markets. Good policies will require knowing about both the type of market failures at play and where they take place.

private and social marginal returns will not in general coincide in a cluster. This, of course, can justify policy intervention and may potentially be supportive of the activism of cluster proponents.

These two conclusions nonetheless come with two strong cautionary warnings regarding policy. First, the fact that many different mechanisms (sharing, matching, and learning) in different markets (labour, intermediates, ideas) can generate local increasing returns, though a very positive result (because one can assume some form of local increasing returns without having to rely on a specific mechanism to explain clustering), implies that identifying the precise sources of clustering will be difficult (Rosenthal and Strange 2004). In turn, the appropriate corrective policies will depend on the exact mechanism(s) at play. For example, the corrective policies associated with local knowledge spillovers are not the same as those stemming from imperfect matching on the labour market. Second, economic agents are not compensated for the positive effects they generate but they also do not have to compensate others for their positive effects. With such reciprocal external effects, it is unclear whether the wedge between private and social returns is positive or negative. For instance, a new specialist input provider may 'steal business' from competition. This implies a transfer of rents and this new entrant may thus receive more than its social marginal product. On the other hand, with knowledge diffusion social returns are likely to exceed private returns because of the lack of reward associated with knowledge diffusion. To be consistent with much of the policy literature, we can assume that social marginal returns in clusters exceed private marginal returns. One may want to take issue with this assumption and argue otherwise. Again, this is only a working assumption providing some a-priori rationale for pro-cluster policies.[11]

Mobility of goods and factors. Assumptions about mobility, both between and within clusters, play a crucial role. These assumptions need to cover the geographical mobility of goods, services, ideas, technologies, and primary factors. To make the strongest possible case for clusters, we can assume that some intermediate goods and services in each activity are immobile and thus available only to those operating in the cluster. Final goods can be taken as perfectly mobile. This is an extreme assumption which ensures that the growth potential of a cluster is not limited by the size of its market. Turning finally to primary factors of production, land is immobile (but may be used for different activities) whereas capital is arguably highly mobile. Labour and firms (and more accurately firms' knowledge) are more complicated cases. As shown below, labour mobility plays a fundamental role, although it is not addressed by the standard recommendations of cluster initiatives.

---

[11] Instead, should private marginal returns exceed social marginal returns, clusters would need to be taxed. Ideally, the case that social returns are below private returns should be made empirically. The prima facie evidence is nonetheless supportive of the assumption made here since part of the surplus made in the cluster will capitalize in land values and thus accrue to inactive landowners.

2.1.3 *The simple mechanics of clusters*

The assumptions described above can now be brought together within a consistent model. This model can be represented diagrammatically.[12]

Productivity curve. The first relationship links the local productivity in an activity to its local employment size.[13] According to the production structure above, the more important an activity is locally, the more productive are the agents involved in it. To be more precise, the productivity of firms in a cluster increases with cluster size because of local increasing returns. The curve in Figure 2.2 (a) represents the productivity that firms in a particular activity face in their cluster as a function of overall employment in the activity in the cluster. This upward-sloping productivity curve stands in sharp contrast with 'neoclassical' productivity curves. In a purely neoclassical environment, cramming more workers and more firms on a fixed amount of land results in decreasing marginal returns so clustering is a very bad idea to start with.

This local productivity relationship is consistent with the observed increase of most measures of local productivity with the local size of a given activity. As will be

---

[12] The graphical device used here is in the spirit of that developed by Combes et al. (2005). The 'modelling' proposed here relies only on diagrams. This is to ease the exposition to the non-technical reader. A formal modelling of the ideas developed here is nonetheless needed (Duranton and Puga 2004).

[13] Employment is taken to be the key measure of cluster size for the sake of the exposition. Other measures like the number of firms could be used. The best way to measure and characterize clusters is discussed in section 4.1.

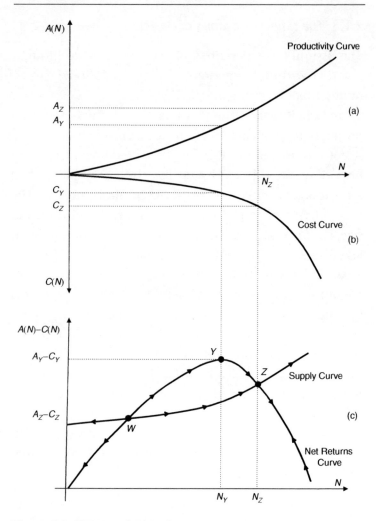

Figure 2.2 Clusters: the baseline case

The Economic Rationale of Clusters

made clear in Chapter 4, there is considerable empirical support for such a relationship. In turn, this increase in efficiency with size can explain the 'localization' of economic activity, i.e. the concentration of a disproportionate share of a given economic activity in a small set of areas. In Figure 2.2 (a), the slope of the productivity curve captures the intensity of the increasing returns in the cluster. The exact shape of the productivity curve depends on the specifics of the mechanism(s) that underpins local increasing returns and is ultimately an empirical issue. Importantly, this shape is expected to differ across activities. Local increasing returns in a textile cluster are unlikely to be driven by the exact same mix of forces as in a bio-tech cluster. These two clusters may then face two very different productivity curves. Furthermore, different clusters in the same activity may also face productivity differences that are unrelated to their size, be it only because some areas may benefit from better natural endowments than others. For instance the northern California wine cluster, all else equal, may be more productive than its upstate New York counterpart for obvious climatic reasons (and less obvious geological reasons).

To be consistent with the priorities of cluster initiatives, our framework represents the mechanics of clusters from the firm's perspective. A more direct focus on workers as in Combes et al. (2005) would lead us to derive a 'wage curve' rather than a productivity curve. This would however change nothing in the reasonings below. In the extreme case where each worker operates his or her own firm, the productivity curve is also a wage curve. In the more plausible case where workers are paid the value of their marginal product or a constant fraction of it, the wage is proportional to productivity (when both are expressed in log). Any wage curve is thus expected to have a very similar shape to the productivity curve represented here.

The cost curve. The second relationship relates the local (marginal) costs of production in an activity to its local employment size. According to the spatial structure above, the amount of available land is limited in any cluster. When the number of firms and employment in the cluster grow, so does the demand for residential and commercial land. Consequently, as a cluster grows, costs are also expected to increase because of higher land prices. As an illustration, two of the largest and most successful clusters in the world, the Silicon Valley (microelectronics and software) and the City of London (finance and business services), have extraordinarily high land costs. The plain line in Figure 2.2 (b) represents the (marginal) costs that firms face in a given activity and cluster as a function of overall employment in this activity in the cluster. For reasons that will soon become obvious, this curve is drawn with a reversed Y-axis.

This increase in the costs of production as a function of size is modelled very simply through the crowding of the land market with a finite supply of land.[14] However, this

[14] An important technical issue needs to be mentioned. An increase in productivity, which raises local incomes, will have a positive effect on the demand for land and thus its price. Hence an upward shift in the

simple relationship can be readily extended to consider a situation where more land is available further away. In this case, an increase in employment would mean a physically larger cluster with greater commuting costs, leading to higher land prices for the central locations. In turn, higher land prices have an effect on the costs of consumption goods through higher retail costs.[15]

Like the productivity curve, the cost relationship has also received some attention in the literature. Its precise shape is also driven by the details of the specific mechanisms that underpin it and is ultimately an empirical matter. Again, like the productivity curve, the cost curve is also expected to differ across activities since land intensity is not the same in all industries. It will also differ across clusters engaged in the same activity because of obvious differences in land availability across areas (not

productivity curve will imply an upward shift in the cost curve. This link is certainly yet another complication that cluster policies will face. However, for the sake of exposition this linkage between these two curves is ignored here. It would be possible, though cumbersome, to consider this link in a more formal model.

[15] Going against this is the fact that a larger market offers a wider variety of suppliers without having to import goods from elsewhere. Since importing goods is costly in terms of transport costs, this effect goes in the opposite direction. A higher level of activity locally may thus imply lower rather than higher costs as argued above. This effect is likely to be important and possibly dominant when one considers very large spatial units for which land issues are of second-order importance. For instance, the 'New Economic Geography' literature (which deals primarily with large spatial units) makes heavy use of this feature (Fujita et al. 1999). For smaller spatial units, however, most goods are imported so that size differences do not matter much in this respect whereas land issues become more prominent (Combes et al. 2005). Hence having costs rise with local employment is an appropriate assumption in the case of clusters, which tend to be relatively small in size as argued below.

to mention institutional differences). Note finally that the cost curve may also reflect a range of market failures associated with the operation of the land market and commuting such as road congestion. The discussion of these complications is postponed to the next section.

The net returns curve. The difference between the productivity curve and the costs curve is represented in Figure 2.2 (c) by the net returns curve. On that figure, this difference is bell-shaped. This corresponds to the case where local increasing returns dominate rising production costs in small clusters, while the reverse occurs in large clusters. For this to be the case, the slope of the productivity curve must be larger than that of the cost curve below a certain threshold, while it is smaller above this threshold. At this threshold, net returns reach their peak (point Y in the figure). This peak can be interpreted as identifying a 'pseudo-optimal' cluster size, which maximizes net returns in the cluster. The reason this is only a 'pseudo-optimum' (also called a constrained optimum in the economics literature) rather than a true optimum is due to the existence of inefficiencies in production. These inefficiencies imply that the productivity curve is not as high as it could be (see below for more).

The supply curve. The second curve represented in Figure 2.2 (c) is a supply curve for labour and firms.[16] This curve indicates for any level of net returns in the

---

[16] For simplicity, labour and firms are thought of as being attached to each other. This could mean that there is a fixed proportion of entrepreneurs in the labour force or, alternatively, that entrepreneurs come with their workers. In reality, attracting labour (and most importantly skilled labour) and firms are two separate problems.

activity, the amount of labour supplied in the cluster. Under perfect labour mobility, the supply curve is flat, that is, if a cluster offers net returns above that of the rest of the economy, there is an infinite supply of new workers willing to move in. A flat supply curve may be an adequate long-run representation for a country with a high level of mobility. However, the time-horizon of cluster initiatives should arguably be the medium run (five to ten years) and not the long run (twenty years or more). Furthermore, in a country like France which we study below, labour is far from being perfectly mobile even over long time periods.[17] As a result we expect the supply curve to be upward-sloping. The steeper the supply curve, the less mobile is less labour. Furthermore, since some clusters may be intrinsically more attractive because of better amenities, this curve may not be the same everywhere. In particular, better amenities will shift this curve *downwards* since workers are willing to accept lower net economic returns in clusters with better amenities.

[17] Labour may be fairly mobile in North America but it is far less so in Europe and elsewhere. Among others, Obstfeld and Peri (1998) estimate that the elasticity of regional migration flows to wage differences is relatively high in the USA but extremely low in Europe. Turning to firms, the evidence is more complex and also more patchy. Direct evidence from Duranton and Puga (2001) who report establishment relocation data for France shows that about 1.5% of the stock of establishments relocate every year. Although nearly three-quarters of relocations are towards clusters, the proportion of relocating establishments is arguably low. Pellenbarg (2005) reports slightly higher numbers for the Netherlands but most of the movements he reports are very short distances. Although systematic direct evidence is still missing, the literature is suggestive of low rates of geographic mobility of existing firms.

Equilibrium. The equilibrium of the model in the absence of any policy intervention can now be derived. This equilibrium corresponds to a situation where workers and firms obtain the returns they need to come and/or stay in the cluster. It is defined by the intersection between the supply curve and the net returns curve. The intersection between these two curves may not be unique. In Figure 2.2 (c), the two curves intersect twice (at W and Z). The supply curve first cuts the net returns curve from above (at W) and then from below (at Z). As made clear by the arrows in the figure, point W is not a stable equilibrium. If the cluster is initially at point W, a small positive employment shock will raise net returns. Higher returns will then attract more firms and workers through the supply curve. This increase in population will lead to another increase in net returns and a further inflow of firms and workers. This movement only stops when the cluster reaches point Z, a stable equilibrium.

Knowing now that point Z is the equilibrium, employment in the cluster can be read at N_Z. Then, the costs of operation and productivity in the cluster can be traced upwards to Figures 2.2 (a) and 2.2 (b) at A_Z and C_Z. Before turning to policy, it remains to show that the cluster will tend to specialize in a single activity (even in absence of policy intervention). To see this, it is useful to consider a hypothetical second activity in the cluster. This second activity has its own productivity curve and a given initial level of employment. The two activities face similar costs since firms and workers are competing for the same land. On the other hand, the two activities face, in general, different productivity levels. In turn productivity differences will imply wage differences between the two activities and workers will leave the activity with the lowest returns and move to the other. This movement ends only when the cluster is specialized in a single activity.[18] More generally, it is inefficient to have 'disjointed' activities in the same place since they bring no benefit to each other and crowd each other's land market.

Thus far, the model shows that employment will have a natural tendency to concentrate in clusters that specialize by activity. There are some productivity benefits associated with this. These benefits are both a cause and a consequence of clustering. It is now possible to examine how the situation can be improved by policy (if at all).

2.1.4 What should cluster policies do?

There are two major inefficiencies associated with clusters in the framework developed here. Let us examine them in turn.

Uncompensated externalities. The first source of inefficiency stems from the production structure. As argued above, the microeconomic foundations of the increasing returns operating inside clusters are all associated with some inefficiencies. First, the indivisibilities at the heart of sharing mechanisms generate a number of

---

[18] Should, for some unspecified reason, the two activities have the exact same returns, a small employment shock, positive or negative, in either of the two activities will again create a small asymmetry between the two activities and lead again to full specialization for the cluster.

inefficiencies. Indivisibilities imply that only a limited number of players will enter. This results in imperfect competition and the (inefficient) exploitation of market power. If new entrants increase the diversity of, say, local inputs, they are unlikely to reap the full benefits of this increase in diversity. We also expect firms to make their entry decision on the basis of the profits they can make rather than the social surplus they create, which under imperfect competition is again inefficient. Second, with matching mechanisms, a different set of inefficiencies will be at play. For instance, firms neglect the positive effects of their vacancies on the job search of workers. Finally, there are also many possible inefficiencies associated with learning mechanisms: with imperfect protection of property rights, firms are likely to invest too little in knowledge generation; in the absence of rewards for knowledge diffusion, too little of it will take place; firms in clusters may be reluctant to train their workers if they expect them to be poached by competition in the future, etc. These are only several of the inefficiencies that can occur when production takes place under increasing returns.[19]

The important point to remember here is that there are possibly a very large number of inefficiencies in the production process. If these inefficiencies were suppressed, productivity would increase in the cluster at any level of employment. Using the same diagrammatic framework, this suggests that there is a potential productivity curve

[19] Duranton and Puga (2004) examine a much longer, but still very incomplete, list.

that the cluster could attain if all the inefficiencies in production were corrected. This potential productivity curve is of course above the productivity curve used previously. It is represented by the dashed line in Figure 2.3 (a). To reach the potential productivity curve rather than the actual one in absence of intervention, the policy must cure *all* the inefficiencies in production so that economic agents face the dashed productivity curve in Figure 2.3 (a).

The major difficulty here is the precise identification of the inefficiencies in production so that the potential productivity curve is reached. To repeat, clustering is driven by a variety of mechanisms whose relative importance is extremely difficult to identify empirically. These mechanisms then all call for different corrective policies. For instance, corrective policies aimed at dealing with labour market matching problems will have nothing to do with those aimed at fostering knowledge diffusion, etc. Put differently, we need some corrective policies for inefficiencies that we know close to nothing about.[20]

Assuming a set of corrective policies can be implemented to reach the potential productivity curve, the equilibrium would be affected in the following way. Subtracting the costs curve (in Figure 2.3 b) from the potential productivity curve yields the potential net returns curve, i.e. the net returns that could be attained in the

[20] Furthermore, these inefficiencies are likely to occur in most places. The fact that they are not dealt with by central governments is possibly an indication of how difficult they are to solve and not a good reason for local authorities to attempt to cure them.

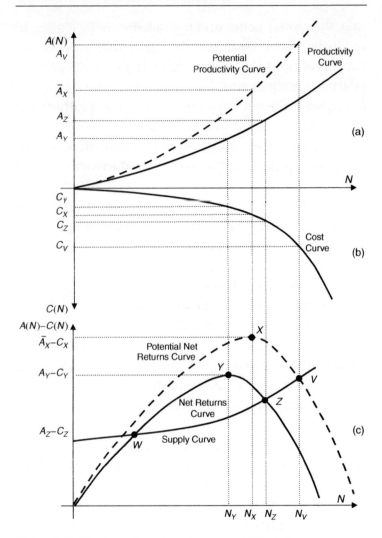

Figure 2.3 Cluster policy when labour mobility is low

absence of inefficiency in production. It is represented by the dashed line in Figure 2.3 (c). On this figure, potential net returns are maximized at $\overline{A}_X - C_X$ for a level of employment N_X (point X). However, the equilibrium does not occur at this point but at point V instead. This suggests that another inefficiency is still at play.

The cluster coordination failure. Hence, after correcting the inefficiencies in production the equilibrium is still inefficient and involves a cluster that is too large with respect to its true optimal size in N_X. More generally, the equilibrium may occur at the optimum only in the particular case for which the degree of labour mobility is such that the supply curve happens to intersect the potential net returns curve exactly at point X. Consequently, when labour is rather mobile, as in the figure, existing clusters are *too large* (even when the inefficiencies in production are fixed). In that case, employment in any activity concentrates into too few clusters which turn out to be too big. Alternatively, labour may be sufficiently immobile for the supply curve to intersect with the net returns curve to the left of the pseudo-optimum. In this alternative case, clusters *appear* to be too small.

Let us remain for now with the case of labour mobility being sufficiently high for clusters to be too big. In this case, there is a coordination failure. All existing clusters are going to be too big. This inefficient situation can be sustained. The main reason is that no one wants to move alone and develop a new cluster because it would mean forming a very small and thus very unproductive cluster. It would be worthwhile to move to a new cluster only if a large enough group of workers and firms decided to coordinate their move. Note that the creation of such a new cluster would be desirable for everyone since existing clusters would become smaller and thus be able to offer higher returns. The problem is of course that, in the absence of policy, there is nothing to coordinate this movement of workers to new clusters.

Hence, the policy conclusion is that existing clusters should restrict their size while empty places should develop new clusters. This conclusion runs contrary to the advice of most cluster proponents for whom bigger clusters always seem to be better. Why do we reach opposite conclusions? It is not because of our assumptions about productivity. Just like most of the cluster literature we have assumed an upward-sloping productivity curve. It is not because of the supply curve and labour mobility either. Cluster proponents do not worry much about labour mobility (if at all) and usually assume implicitly that it is relatively high. In fact, we reach a different conclusion only because we have (realistically) considered a negative feedback whereby clusters get increasingly crowded as they grow.[21]

Assuming labour is sufficiently mobile, the key practical difficulty is to locate point X. Since the level of employment associated with maximized returns depends on a curve that is unknown (the *potential* productivity curve) and a curve that is possibly very difficult to estimate (the cost curve), it is very hard to know for

[21] And such a limit to cluster size is needed, otherwise each activity would end up concentrating in only one cluster in equilibrium.

which level of employment the difference between the two curves will be maximized.

Cluster policies when labour mobility is low. Let us now turn to this alternative case. Figure 2.4 (c) represents a situation where the supply curve intersects with the potential net returns curve from below before its peak. The equilibrium in the absence of any corrective policy is at point Z and entails clusters which are smaller than they would be in Y. Even after fixing the inefficiencies in production, the equilibrium in V still entails clusters smaller than in X, the maximum of the potential net returns curve.

The fact that clusters are smaller than the size that would maximize net returns does not mean that a policy focused on cluster growth is desirable. Quite the contrary, the cluster is too small because mobility is very costly. Hence making a cluster grow will also be very costly. When labour and firms are highly mobile it may make sense to propose some subsidies to attempt to attract more workers and firms. For the low mobility case represented in Figure 2.4 (c), point V is the best the cluster can hope to achieve after having corrected the market failures in production. Attempting to reach point X makes no sense since the cost of the subsidy would outweigh the benefits from higher net returns.[22]

Hence cluster growth policies are not desirable when labour mobility is low. In conclusion, either labour is

---

[22] The deadweight loss of getting from point V to point X is the area below the supply curve and above the potential net returns curve. In the present case, it is likely to be very large.

The Economic Rationale of Clusters

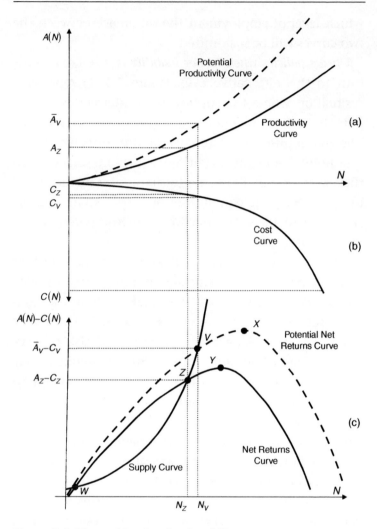

Figure 2.4 Clusters' low levels of mobility

sufficiently mobile and clusters are expected to be too big or labour is not sufficiently mobile and clusters may be too small. In the first situation cluster growth policies are obviously wrong-headed while in the second they are not worth pursuing because of their high cost. In this latter case, the policy recommendation is instead to increase labour mobility and thus make the supply curve flatter so that it intersects with the net returns curve closer to its maximum.

With respect to this recommendation, an added complication is that the supply curve itself may be subject to some market failures. Put differently, there may be some inefficiency that makes the supply curve too steep (or too flat). For instance, imperfect information about wages and cost of living can make risk-averse workers reluctant to move to a cluster. Although the empirical evidence concerning market failures associated with internal migration is still very sketchy, there is strong evidence of regulatory barriers to mobility (Greenwood 1997). The myriad of small (and sometimes big) barriers to internal mobility that have been documented include public housing when allocated by a queuing system, the workings of unemployment agencies, the high taxes when buying or selling a house in some countries, etc.

Hence, when labour mobility is low three complications arise: (i) the coordination failure that makes clusters too big may be absent; (ii) however, it is hard to know if labour mobility is low enough to lead to this type of situation in reality; (iii) but when this is the case offering subsidies to attract firms and workers would then be pointless; and finally (iv) the mobility of firms and workers may be subject to market failures. In addition to this, local governments should be wary of dealing with market failures associated with the mobility of firms and workers since what may lower the cost of attracting workers to a cluster may also lower their cost of leaving that cluster. On the other hand, central governments may face large efficiency gains from improved internal mobility. Despite 2006 having been the 'European Year of Worker Mobility' for the European Union, European governments are very reluctant to take any step to reduce existing barriers to mobility. A simple reason behind this lack of action is the fact that increasing mobility is likely to create both winning and losing clusters. If a steep supply curve like that in Figure 2.4 is made much flatter (as in Figure 2.2), this raises efficient cluster size from N_V to N_X. If total employment in the activity remains unchanged at the aggregate level, having bigger clusters also means having fewer of them.

In conclusion, the policy recommendations derived here differ quite significantly from those of cluster proponents despite very similar starting points. There are two main differences. First, the vast array of policies that are often recommended for cluster upgrading by cluster proponents seem only vaguely related to the market failures associated with clustering. Some of the recommendations of Porter (2000b) such as specialized training, university research efforts, or specialized transportation infrastructure are very expensive items. This may be a lot of money spent for unlikely solutions to ill-identified market failures.[23] Second, recall that Porter (2000b)'s objective is to increase both size and productivity (or, equivalently, increase productivity both directly and indirectly through a larger size). It is as if the model he had in mind was only the top part of Figure 2.3 and the objective was to move rightwards along the productivity curve as well as somehow shift it upwards. As made clear by parts (b) and (c) of the figure, this is not an adequate policy.

2.2 Clusters in a more realistic world

Despite using a very simple framework, the previous section has shown that cluster initiatives as often advocated have a very ambiguous rationale. When rigorously followed through, the policy recommendations derived from cluster theory seem far less appealing than cluster proponents would like us to believe. As shown in this section, the problems only worsen when one tries to make the theoretical framework more realistic.

2.2.1 Congestion and other frictions

After observing the complications induced by a more realistic supply curve, we can now turn to those associated with a more realistic approach to the cost curve.

---

[23] This statement does not mean that training or higher education should not be of concern to policy makers. These interventions are criticized here as tools to foster clusters.

In the baseline case, costs are simply assumed to increase with cluster employment following the crowding of the local land market. The implicit assumption made in the baseline case is that private marginal costs (those paid by producers) were equal to social marginal costs (the costs to the economy). With a perfectly functioning land market and in the absence of congestion, this equality between private and social marginal costs holds naturally. Empirically, we expect neither of these two assumptions to hold. Land markets are subject to significant frictions and are strongly regulated through planning and zoning regulations. Congestion in local transportation is also pervasive when clusters start growing.

A first implication of congestion and frictions on the land market is that the cost curve in the absence of policy is distorted. With proper corrective policies, it should be possible to reduce costs for any level of employment in the cluster. For instance, a congestion tax could reduce the level of congestion in the cluster and increase total surplus. In the diagrams used so far (e.g. Figure 2.4), this suggests that we should also consider a potential cost curve that stands above the cost curve in the absence of policy intervention (keeping in mind that the vertical axis is reversed in the middle part of the figure). Potentially lower costs would then mean an even higher potential net returns curve in the lower part of the figure. Depending on the shape of the potential cost curve relative to the cost curve in absence of policy, optimal cluster size may increase or decline. Hence, considering some obvious complications associated with the imperfections of the land market and commuting generates yet further complications for cluster policies.

Second, there is another subtlety that cluster proponents do not appear to acknowledge: cluster policies may conflict with other local public policies.[24] Porter's motto involves 'removing obstacles, relaxing constraints, and eliminating inefficiencies' (Porter 2000b, 26). In turn, this leads to a vast array of policy measures to improve 'competitiveness' (see for instance Porter (2000b, 30–2). Assuming that the absence of any mention of the land market in the writings of Porter is an oversight, 'removing obstacles' and 'relaxing constraints' should also apply to local zoning and planning regulations.[25] Scrapping planning and zoning regulations may be harmful. Although the effects of zoning and planning regulations are intensely debated in the literature (Fischel 2000), a case can be made that they can improve the quality of life for local residents. For instance, although the land use regulations in the Bay area around San Francisco appear suboptimal to many observers, the quality of life around San Francisco would in all likelihood decline if all 'obstacles' and 'constraints' on

[24] Distributional issues are also ignored by cluster proponents. A successful cluster policy is unlikely to create only winners. Residents on fixed incomes will lose from any increase in local land prices associated with cluster growth.

[25] This absence is conspicuous in the writings examined here. There is a similar absence in Sölvell et al. (2003) and most of the cluster policy literature. The report by the UK Department of the Environment, Transport, and the Regions (2000) is an exception though it approaches land issues very differently.

land use were to be removed. Put differently, efforts to strengthen clusters may clash with other other existing policies and cluster proponents do not offer any guidance about how to resolve these conflicts.

2.2.2 Cluster policy in a dynamic setting

The analysis so far has been mostly static in nature. This contrasts with the emphasis of Porter and many of his followers on the dynamic dimensions of 'competitiveness' such as innovation and productivity growth. However, it can first be argued that much of this prominence given to the rate of growth is unwarranted. To understand why, it can be noted that increasing the annual rate of growth of local productivity by, say, one-fifth would constitute a very successful productivity growth policy.[26] With productivity growing at around 2 per cent per year (and often less), this enormously successful policy would only mean an extra 0.4 per cent per year. For the cumulative effects of such policy to become sizeable and generate a gain in levels of, say, 10 per cent, one would need to wait for nearly twenty-five years. In contrast, reducing urban congestion or improving local infrastructure may have an equally large effect within months rather than years. So, despite the

[26] Despite productivity growth being the major focus of UK economic policies since 1997, the evidence of faster productivity growth in this country is yet to materialize. See for instance the chapters in Department of Trade and Industry (2001b).

insistence of cluster proponents on dynamic aspects, static effects as discussed above do matter.[27]

The second response is that considering explicitly dynamic issues introduces yet further complications to cluster policies. The life-cycle of clusters is the fundamental issue here. It begs two key questions. First, can clusters be created from scratch? Second, what should a cluster policy be like if clusters may come and go?

To answer the first question, the policy literature is divided. Porter clearly states that 'there should be some seeds of a cluster that have passed the market test before cluster developments efforts are justified' (Porter 2000b: 26). Many cluster initiatives are not as cautious and often propose to develop new clusters from scratch. Software, microelectronics, and bio-technology are usually the industry of choice.

Empirically, Porter's caution seems to be warranted. Even though the knowledge-base of a cluster might be expanded, it cannot be created out of nothing. This difficulty of replicating clusters can be explained by the fact that cutting-edge knowledge at the technological frontier in most activities is mainly tacit and spread across a large number of workers. This immobility of cutting-edge knowledge (at least in the short run) has been evidenced in a number of ways. For instance, the literature on

---

[27] Cluster proponents may respond that what they call 'dynamic effects' would encompass any improvement in productivity rather than only improvements in the rate of productivity growth. In such a case, however, the discussion of the previous section can no longer be dismissed for being 'static'. Furthermore, giving such a broad meaning to the word 'dynamic' would make it useless as a qualifier.

patent citations finds strong localization effects whereby new patents tend to rely disproportionately on previous innovations that were developed nearby (see section 4.1 for more on this). In a very different vein, van der Linde (2003) finds evidence of only one case of successful cluster creation by policy (Hinshu in Taiwan) in a survey of more than 700 clusters. One of the 'fathers' of the Silicon Valley, Frederick Terman, who as dean of engineering and provost of Stanford University oversaw the creation and development of Silicon Valley, was unable to replicate this again in the highly favourable environment of New Jersey some years later when poached by Bell Labs (Leslie and Kargon 1996).

However, the fact that today's cutting-edge knowledge is not mobile does not imply that clusters will remain what they are and where they are forever. The reason is that the current frontier of knowledge will eventually be pushed forward and the creation of a new generation of cutting-edge knowledge may happen elsewhere. When George Eastman revolutionized the photographic industry in Rochester (NY), the latter city took over from New York as the main cluster for the industry. After the emulsion coating technology was in turn made obsolete by the digital revolution in photography, Rochester lost much of its prominence in this industry. The systematic evidence in Arzaghi and Davis (2005) and Duranton (2007) shows that this example is not an isolated case but representative of a pattern. Activities move around, sometimes quite a lot. Worse, the more high-tech and clustered industries (often cherished by cluster proponents) seem to be even more mobile (Arzaghi and Davis 2005). Hence, increasing clustering means increasing the risk exposure of the local economy. Besides, trying to glue activities somewhere may be futile (as was Eastman-Kodak's attempt to resist the digital revolution in photography). This resistance may even be socially harmful since it can slow down the development of better alternatives elsewhere.[28] A good case can be made that great cities are great not because they have managed to keep their leadership in one activity since the dawn of time but because they have managed to periodically reinvent themselves after losing an important part of their economic fabric. Boston is a case in point (Glaeser 2005).

In summary, taking a more dynamic perspective complicates the problem of cluster policies even further by underscoring uncertainties about how long an activity can stay in a given cluster.

In addition dynamic considerations may also play an important role when workers are less than perfectly mobile. A geography organized in industrial clusters is also a risky geography: industrial clusters have existed since the industrial revolution but the decline of certain sectors—steel, textiles etc.—has translated into a decline of certain regions that had their fate tied to

---

[28] At the early phases of their development, alternative technologies and designs are often not obviously superior to existing products. For instance mechanical calculators were produced for many years after the development of the first electronic calculators. Trying to strengthen the mechanical calculator cluster around London in the 1970s would have been a mistake for the London region and might have harmed the development of a new industry that tremendously reduced the cost of basic computations.

a single sector. The large agglomerations have survived and developed thanks to diversified economic structure. It is impossible today to determine which sectors will be the declining ones tomorrow. Globalization has certainly increased this uncertainty and the risk of territorial specialization. Labour immobility makes the problem worse since a sectoral decline that transforms into a regional decline will not generate sufficient migration of workers towards the more dynamic regions. It is widely accepted today that the education system should not lead to over-specialization of young workers because the sector-specific skills may easily become obsolete in case of negative sectoral shocks. It is not clear why this type of reasoning should not apply for regions as well. Of course, the conclusion is not that regional specialization should be deterred by public policies: specialized clusters have economic benefits that are quantified later in the report. The risk of specialization, even in high-tech sectors, should however be well understood. The danger of cluster policies that would tend to artificially specialize regions should therefore be clear. One policy implication to which we will come back is that labour mobility should be encouraged in Europe. The main challenge is not to increase migration between countries but inside countries. It would have two benefits in connection to clusters. By making labour supply more elastic, higher worker mobility would facilitate the 'natural' development of clusters. It would also make workers less vulnerable to sectoral shocks that become regional shocks in a geography organized in clusters.

2.2.3 *When cluster policies can turn ugly: political economy*

The argument so far is that even if the public authority that oversees the cluster is highly competent and attempts to maximize local welfare, an optimal cluster policy looks like something extraordinarily difficult to achieve. Now, two further questions need to be addressed. Are those in charge of cluster policies really able to pursue them competently? And if so, are they trying to maximize social welfare? To answer the first question, it should be noted that in most countries cluster policies are conducted in a highly decentralized manner by sub-national governments or by some mix of sub-national government and semi-autonomous bodies representing the actors of the cluster. In most cases sub-national levels of governments do not have the capabilities to design complex economic development policies. They naturally call upon consultants to help them. The shortfalls of the conceptual frameworks used by these consultants are not encouraging for the possibility of successful cluster policies. Turning to the second question, there is a very large political economy literature that shows how and why governments cannot be expected to be fully benevolent (Besley 2006).

The fact that the institutions in charge of cluster policies may not be entirely competent nor fully benevolent may seem like a truism since these two caveats apply to most, if not all, policies. They are, however, especially important in the case of cluster policies. A lack of competence can be expected to matter more for complex policies such as cluster initiatives. A lack of benevolence is also especially damaging here. This is because when it comes to clusters, there is a double asymmetry of information. The producers in a cluster will know more about their activity, their level of performance, and the local prospects than the authority in charge of cluster policies. In turn, the local policy makers will know much more than their voters. These asymmetries of information can be detrimental in a number of ways.

The worst possible situation occurs when a group of industries collude with their local authority and use a cluster initiative as a way to extract resources for themselves. Although this case of industries and politicians explicitly ganging up against the public might be rare, at least in developed countries, two other more plausible situations can be envisioned.

First, politicians may use cluster initiatives to raise their profile with the passive complicity of the beneficiary industries. While some of the activity of local authorities is easy to monitor by voters, a lot of what they do is much harder to assess. On the one hand, uncollected garbage, for example, is for everyone to notice (and to smell). On the other hand, a transit choice between a subway system and an increased supply of buses in dedicated lanes is much harder to evaluate. In this case, we expect the political bias to favour the more 'visible' projects. In the public transport example used above, subway lines get built over and over again despite, in most cases, their appalling economic record (Gomez-

Ibanez 1996). Similarly, between a number of small and potentially beneficial local initiatives like an improvement in the planning process or improving local amenities and something more shiny like trying to attract bio-tech firms, the political choice will often be biased in favour of the latter, however low its probability of success. In some respect, cluster initiatives are even more appealing than major infrastructure projects since it is easy to exaggerate their scope. The fanfare with which a national cluster initiative was launched in France a few years ago is a good example of this type of bias.

A second type of situation that we also expect to encounter frequently is the 'capture' of governments by industries. Following Baldwin and Robert-Nicoud (2007), an interesting version of the capture argument is that we expect declining industries rather than more dynamic ones to benefit from cluster initiatives. The reason is that it is in badly performing clusters that producers have the strongest incentives to convince local authorities that they need a cluster initiative. In more dynamic industries, the opportunity cost of lobbying is higher. Unfortunately, the lobbying effort by poorly performing industries also implies diverting resources from the development of their productive capabilities. This idea that cluster initiatives may be targeted at losers is consistent with many of our findings below.

In conclusion, cluster policies that already look fraught with difficulties in a world of benevolent governments look extremely unappealing when political agency is explicitly taken into account.

2.3 Some elements towards local economic development policies

The theoretical framework presented earlier was used to highlight the inadequacies of cluster policies. This section shows which 'positive' policy lessons may be learnt from it. Since this model is very crude, these policy recommendations are very sketchy and do not constitute a detailed blueprint for local economic development. They nevertheless provide a broad framework within which local development policies can be examined.[29]

2.3.1 'Pay more attention to the cost curve than the productivity curve'

In relation to Figure 2.2, cluster policies appear to focus mostly on the productivity curve and neglect the complications associated with the cost curve and supply curve below. In this respect, cluster initiatives are not very different from a number of other policy recommendations for local development that have surfaced in the last twenty years such as fostering 'learning regions' (Morgan 1997) or attracting the 'high bohemians' of the creative class (Florida 2002), etc.

This near-exclusive focus on the productivity curve is misplaced. In the case of cluster proponents, this is because the policies are just too hard to design and implement, while their possible gains are elusive.

[29] See Combes et al. (2005) for more on this.

Moreover, a good case can be made that productivity policies are probably best left to central governments.[30] Instead, larger gains can be achieved locally by improving the policies associated with the cost curve, such as land-use planning, urban transport, provision of local public goods, etc. These policies, which have been for the longest time the 'staple' policies of local governments, may not be as 'sexy' as setting up a bio-tech cluster or the next Silicon Valley. They are nonetheless fundamental determinants of how easy it is to produce in a place and how pleasant it is to live there.

Still, good policies associated with the cost curve are difficult to achieve.[31] For instance, urban transport policies raise many tough questions. What should downtown parking provision be like? Should there be a congestion tax? Should the supply of taxis be regulated? If

[30] A higher productivity often materializes in lower prices which benefit all consumers while local producers may not benefit much. Hence local policies may not be a good idea when the benefits are so broadly distributed. Besides, the market failures that can justify those productivity policies take place everywhere so that a common (i.e. national) set of corrective policies may be desirable.

[31] One may also worry whether correcting inefficiencies on the cost side makes sense in light of the inefficiencies associated with the productivity curve. First, it is unlikely that fixing local congestion will make the other inefficiencies so much worse as to lower net returns. Using Figure 2.2, it is true that one local authority in isolation will not improve net returns by lowering local costs. This is because any gain on the cost side will lead to the arrival of newcomers and net returns remain equal to $A_Z - C_Z$. This complete crowding out of the costs improvement is caused by perfect labour mobility. From Figure 2.4, lower costs lead to an increase in net returns in absence of perfect mobility. Besides, as exposed below, if many jurisdictions lower their costs, the net returns will improve in many places and this will lead to a higher supply curve and thus a better allocation in the economy.

so, how? Should new roads be built? Should the public transit network be extended? How should it be priced? Are the latest traffic management technologies worth the investment? All these questions (and many more) are hard to answer. Despite all this, a good transport policy is easier to implement than a good cluster policy.[32] This is because we know a lot more about the inefficiencies of urban traffic than those taking place in local production. Furthermore, a bad transport policy is often for all to observe unlike a bad cluster policy.

Finally, when they try to develop clusters and interfere with the local composition of economic activity, local authorities are likely to overreach themselves. Given their limited capabilities, local government may spread themselves too thin by trying to do too much.[33] This may have a negative impact on their other policies. To conclude, the recommendation for local governments is thus to improve their traditional areas of intervention rather than try to do 'new things'.

2.3.2 'Go for growth, sometimes'

The second set of local policies has to do with the supply curve. Although some cities may be too big, in a world

[32] This does not prevent local government from getting their transport policies spectacularly wrong sometimes, as Paris did recently (Prud'homme et al. 2005).

[33] Focusing the effort on the cost curve does not imply that local authorities should always try to micro-manage everything. A good case may be made that local authorities should be more involved in the details of traffic management and possibly less so in some of the details of land use.

of upward-sloping supply curves as in Figure 2.4, most places may be too small.[34] These raises two questions. Does 'going for growth' make sense? And if so, how should it be done?

To answer the first question, being bigger does yield some economic benefits (despite the reluctance to admit it in some quarters). These benefits from size are often called 'urbanization economies'. They can be measured using the same regression approach used to measure the benefits from clustering. There is a vigourous academic debate about the elasticity of local wages and local productivity with respect to total employment. The current consensus is that, in terms of elasticities, urbanization effects are about as large as clustering or localization effects (Rosenthal and Strange 2004; Combes et al. 2008). Even though the elasticities are about the same, a larger size seems to be more desirable than increased specialization for several reasons. First, the contribution of size to local productivity and wages is much larger than that of specialization (Ciccone and Hall 1996; Combes et al. 2008) with a much higher partial R^2 in the regressions. Then, it is arguably much easier to 'go for growth' (i.e. increase local employment irrespective of sector) than expand employment in a particular activity. Finally, diversified growth is less risky than increased cluster specialization.

However, going for growth is no panacea. In particular, there is a sharp trade-off in some places between

[34] It might be argued that many Western European countries such as France, Italy, Spain, and the UK have too few big cities.

employment and population growth, on the one hand, and local amenities, on the other. Unsurprisingly, many places with outstanding amenities (from San Francisco to central Paris) have implemented very restrictive policies instead of going for further growth. Again, one may take issue with the way those restrictive policies are implemented and criticize their excessive restrictiveness. However, there is very little doubt that central Paris would lose much of its valuable charm if development were allowed to proceed unfettered.

Should the case for growth be strong enough (and it appears to be quite strong in many places), how should growth be fostered? However 'policy incorrect' this may sound, the recent literature appears to indicate that the recipe for growth involves being attractive, sprawly, and opportunistic. Attractive means providing good local amenities from parks and safety to good primary schools. It is hard to assess the local growth effects of better amenities in general. Studies that concentrate on climate find that nice weather is a first-order determinant of local growth (Rappaport 2007). It is of course hard to affect local climate.[35] But other amenities can be improved by local policies.

There is also mounting evidence showing that cities exhibiting more of what is often referred to pejoratively as urban sprawl may enjoy better outcomes (Glaeser and Kahn 2001, 2004) and possibly faster growth

[35] The fact that climate is exogenous makes it easier to assess it as a determinant of local growth. Assessing the effect of other amenities is plagued by endogeneity problems.

(Baum-Snow 2007). This should not come as a surprise. Cities that offer their residents the type of housing they like and easy commutes to jobs should fare better than those that prevent newcomers from settling in and offer inconvenient commutes.[36] However, 'be sprawly' does not mean that a free-for-all type of development is desirable. Recall that the first recommendation is to be attractive.[37] Most places need to achieve a balance between preservation (environmental or architectural) and affordable housing (and urban efficiency more generally). This balance will differ across places. However a good case can be made that too many places are too restrictive (see Glaeser et al. 2006 for the USA and Cheshire and Sheppard 2002 for the UK).

Back to the baseline model, the rationale for being attractive is that better amenities lower the supply curve. For sprawl, affordable housing and easy commutes raise the cost curve (i.e. they lower local costs). In light of this framework, the reasons for 'opportunism' are also easy to understand when the supply curve is less than perfectly elastic. Employment growth is hard to boost in 'normal conditions' since established firms are nearly immobile and start-ups take many years to develop (if ever). Newly created large establishments searching for

[36] This is consistent with the recommendation above regarding the focus on the cost curve.

[37] Although sprawliness and attractiveness may conflict at times, a city can manage both. Portland and Seattle score very high on the sprawl measure of Burchfield et al. (2006). These cities are nonetheless widely viewed as attractive. At the opposite end, Detroit is both compact and often deemed not very attractive.

a location represent quick opportunities for significant employment growth. Such growth opportunities do not come for free, however, because there are usually a number of jurisdictions competing for them. This brings us to the last recommendation.

2.3.3 'Central governments, let them compete'

The argument developed here against cluster policies could be viewed as part of a broader argument against territorial competition. The latter is usually regarded with much suspicion in the academic literature (Cheshire and Gordon 1998). The case against territorial competition, as made in the literature, is in two parts. First, territorial competition is accused of being at best a zero-sum game. Since the establishment needs to locate somewhere (so goes the argument), there is no social gain from territorial competition, only losses due to the cost of competing. Although it is true that the competition process may be costly (cost of learning about existing opportunities, bidding, etc.), we also expect large new plants to generate positive local external effects (by the same logic exposed above for clustering). The crucial point is that these external effects can vary across places. In the absence of territorial competition, plants may end up in the 'wrong' location.[38] With territorial competition, the places for which the external effects are the strongest are expected to bid the most. Hence, at the

[38] In the absence of territorial competition, plants choose their location so as to maximize their *private* profit, ignoring external effects.

(modest) cost of the competition process, territorial competition can improve the spatial allocation of plants.

The second part of the traditional case against territorial competition stems from its (possibly large) redistributive element (from places to firms) with places paying 'too much' to get the plants. While there is certainly a theoretical possibility of a 'curse of the winner' associated with this type of rivalry, the social gain (or loss) of the winner is ultimately an empirical question.[39] This is very hard to investigate because of the very large number of confounding factors that can explain the evolution of the places that get these plants. In a very clever recent piece, Greenstone and Moretti (2004) gathered data about not only the winners of a large number of such contests, but also their 'runners-up' (jurisdictions that also bid and came close to winning but ultimately lost). Since the runners-up are arguably very similar *ex ante* to the winners, *ex post* differences are very likely to be mostly due to winning or losing such a contest. The comparison of the winners and runners-up, before and after, is suggestive of sizeable local gains associated with the successful attraction of new plants.[40]

This argument in favour of territorial competition is actually broader than the narrow issue of bidding for new plants. To avoid the pitfalls of cluster policies, there is a temptation to restrict the powers of local governments

[39] Notwithstanding the fact that these transfers may increase aggregate investment and improve its efficiency.

[40] These bids are not usually part of cluster strategies. They belong instead to broad-based policies that attempt to promote local growth or reverse local decline.

with respect to local development or instead conduct cluster policies at the national level as in France. Both temptations should be resisted. National cluster policies are subject to many of the same problems as local cluster initiatives. Government failures may be even more serious with centralized cluster policies because of the political pressure to spread the subsidies across the country.[41] This runs against the strong concentration tendencies at the heart of the benefits from clustering. Despite the strong case developed here against cluster policies, preventing local governments from being in charge of their destinies would be wrong.[42]

In a large majority of jurisdictions in developed economies we expect homeowners to form a majority and elect local officials acting in their interest. In practice, this implies trying to maximize aggregate land values in their jurisdiction. In the absence of strong interdependencies across jurisdictions, this local maximization of land values can lead to efficient outcomes. In brief, we expect local characteristics such as good amenities or high wages to be capitalized into land values. Since land prices reflect how much residents and firms are willing

[41] The recent French cluster policy that subsidizes more than 60 cluster efforts across the country is a case in point.

[42] Although this piece is very critical of cluster policies and raises more general doubts about other types of local 'productivity' policies, it does not advocate curtailing the power of local authorities in matters of local economic development. For instance, local governments can act as a catalyst (and no more) between local producers and universities at very low cost. Despite the scepticism expressed here, it might also be that a local government will some day find a 'good formula' for local economic development that can then be applied elsewhere.

to pay to be somewhere, maximizing land values can be synonymous with the maximization of the attractiveness of a place.[43]

We return to Figure 2.2. As local governments try to maximize their land values and the attractiveness of their own jurisdiction, they also shift the supply curve of other jurisdictions upwards. In turn, to avoid an exodus these other jurisdictions need to offer a 'better deal' to their residents. In practice, a better deal can mean a higher quality of life (through a lowering of costs and better amenities) or higher incomes and more economic opportunities (through a growth strategy). Then, and as can be seen from Figure 2.2, a higher supply curve reduces the inefficiency associated with the cluster coordination failure. Put differently, with the natural tendency of local economies to specialize (at least some of them, as shown above), territorial competition should lead to more efficient clusters without any direct intervention into the production process by local authorities.

Many may disagree with this sketch (or think there is much to disagree with in it). However, the main point to remember is that local government should focus on the issues for which they can make a valuable difference. This means a concentration on the policies associated with their cost curve rather than their productivity curve, and deciding whether they want to go for growth

---

[43] This increase in land prices can then be taxed away to ensure an optimal provision of local public goods. It is beyond the scope of this chapter to enter the detail of this argument. See Becker and Henderson (2000) and Wildasin (2002) for recent complete treatments. These ideas date back to George (1884) and Tiebout (1956).

or preservation. For central governments, who should take a national approach to productivity-related issues, the focus should be on the governance of their sub-national units and how the latter should compete.

Clusters are a complex second-order issue that wrongly receives first-order attention. More specifically, the case against cluster policies is in two parts. First, good cluster policies involve solving a very difficult coordination problem and correcting for a number of market failures which we know very little about. Adding to the difficulty, cluster policies need to be designed and implemented in very uncertain environments without being captured by special interests. Second, even if the policy makers can get it right, as we show in Chapter 4, the benefits of clustering are simply too small empirically to justify significant and sustained efforts towards clusters. Californian clusters may be very prosperous but most clusters are not particularly so. Instead of dreaming about them local policy makers should focus their attention away from the local production structure and aim instead at a more efficient provision of public goods that serve the needs of both residents and a broad range of local producers.

3

The Evolution of French Economic Geography

Before turning to the analysis of the possible gains from cluster policies, it is useful to describe some stylized facts about economic geography and its evolution in France. This also helps us understand whether policies in favour of clusters are simply pushing in the direction of the wind or are going against it. To describe the evolution of economic geography, economists can use several indicators that measure spatial concentration of economic activities. The two measures most often used are the Gini coefficient and the Ellison–Glaeser index (Ellison and Glaeser 1997). In this section, we look at the evolution of these two indices for France over the period 1984–2004.

3.1 Gini and Ellison–Glaeser: definitions

The Gini and Ellison–Glaeser indices do not provide the same type of information on spatial economic concentration. The first one is very descriptive and simply compares the observed distribution of economic activities on the territory to a uniform distribution. It does not fully describe the behaviour of producers. In particular, it does not take into account the industrial concentration of the sector. A sector could be spatially concentrated and have a high Gini coefficient not because firms have decided to locate in a limited number of regions but because the sector is highly concentrated in the sense that it is made of a small number of firms. The Ellison–Glaeser index allows us to take into account and correct for the observed industrial concentration of the sector.

Using our French data set on the 1984–2004 period we computed Gini and Ellison–Glaeser coefficients for each sector and each year.

We use the annual business surveys for industrial sectors from 1984 to 2004 at the plant level. The data are available for plants belonging to firms with more than twenty employees only. We can compute the concentration indices (Gini and Ellison–Glaeser) for different levels of sectoral aggregation (Naf220 and Naf60[1]) at the level of the 'employment area'[2] and of the administrative département. Employment areas (341 in continental France) are typically smaller than départements (94 in continental France).

As shown by Briant et al. (2010), the measure of geographic concentration is potentially affected by the

---

[1] Respectively 88 and 19 industrial sectors in our data set.
[2] Employment areas are defined on the basis of workers' commuting.

shape of the geographic unit which is chosen. This problem is known under the name of *Modifiable Areal Unit Problem* (*MAUP*).

We have computed the Spearman rank correlation for both concentration indices between employment zones and départements and found a very high level (between 87 per cent and 97 per cent). Hence, we conclude that the results we present are not sensitive to the choice of unit.

When we compute the Spearman rank correlation between the Gini and Ellison–Glaeser concentration indices, however, the level of correlation is much weaker (between 52 per cent and 66 per cent).

Hence, correcting for sectoral concentration has potentially important consequences. The Gini and Ellison–Glaeser tell us different things about economic geography, both interesting. The former tells us about the economic geography of economic activities and the second tells more about the choice to locate close to other firms in the same sector.

3.2 The evolution of concentration in France during the past twenty years

Whatever the choice of geographic scale and of sectoral aggregation, more than 60 per cent of sectors experienced an increase in geographic concentration when looking at the Gini coefficient. The conclusion is a bit different for the Ellison–Glaeser coefficient. The share of sectors that experienced an increase in concentration is

Table 3.1 Evolution of concentration: Gini index for 1984–2004 period

	Gini Dept/Naf60	Gini ZE/Naf60	Gini Dept/Naf220	Gini ZE/Naf220
Rank correlation 1984/2004	0.85	0.85	0.85	0.89
Average growth rate of the index	−2.59	−0.37	1.22	1.26
Median growth rate of the index	1.13	1.13	2.44	1.71
% of sectors with positive growth rate of index	0.63	0.67	0.62	0.69

Table 3.2 Evolution of concentration: Ellison–Glaeser index for 1984–2004 period

	Ellison–Glaeser Dept/Naf60	Ellison–Glaeser ZE/Naf60	Ellison–Glaeser Dept/Naf220	Ellison–Glaeser ZE/Naf220
Rank correlation 1984/2004	0.77	0.7	0.73	0.7
Average growth rate of the index	−0.82	−0.36	−0.69	−0.52
Median growth rate of the index	−0.17	0.03	−0.12	−0.12
% of sectors with positive growth rate of index	0.41	0.52	0.45	0.44

almost always less than 50 per cent. The average growth rate is actually negative in all cases. From this point of view, the conclusion is that the choice of firms in the manufacturing activity has been to a small decrease in concentration. The contradiction between the messages brought by the two indices is only apparent. The Gini index is mostly descriptive: it simply says that industrial activities have been more concentrated in the past twenty years. But the analysis of the Ellison–Glaeser index shows that this concentration is due to the industrial concentration of the sector rather than a choice to locate close to other producers in the same sector.

3.3 What explains these evolutions?

3.3.1 Correlation coefficients

Do sectors that concentrate geographically have particular characteristics? To answer this question, we analyse the correlation between the growth rate of each index between 1984 and 2004 and a certain number of sectoral variables. See Tables 3.3 and 3.4.

The growth rate of the Gini coefficient is always negatively correlated with the growth of employment in the sector. This correlation is statistically significant. At the more aggregated level (Naf60), the evolution of the Gini coefficient is also negatively correlated with sales, value added, and exports growth rates. Sectors that lose jobs and are in decline are those that concentrate. However,

Table 3.3 Correlation between growth rate of the Gini index of the sector and growth rate of sectoral variables for the period 1984–2004

	Gini Dept/Naf60	Gini ZE/Naf60	Gini Dept/Naf220	Gini ZE/Naf220
Employment	−0.43*	−0.56*	−0.20*	−0.21*
Sales	−0.45*	−0.50*	−0.10	−0.09
Value added	−0.34	−0.44*	−0.10	−0.09
Exports	−0.42*	−0.50*	−0.15	−0.15
Share of exports in sales	−0.17	−0.22	−0.39*	−0.36*
Average wages	0.028	0.01	0.04	0.04
Productivity	0.12	0.14	−0.03	−0.00
Profit	0.18	0.19	−0.04	0.05

Note: Coefficients that are statistically significant at 5% are signalled by *.

Table 3.4 Correlation between growth rate of the Ellison–Glaeser index of the sector and growth rate of sectoral variables for the period 1984–2004

	Ellison–Glaeser Dept/Naf60	Ellison–Glaeser ZE/Naf60	Ellison–Glaeser Dept/Naf220	Ellison–Glaeser ZE/Naf220
Employment	0.20	0.03	0.01	−0.01
Sales	0.15	0.26	−0.02	−0.03
Value added	0.17	0.21	−0.03	−0.03
Exports	0.63*	0.14	−0.07	−0.04
Share of exports in sales	0.56*	0.07	−0.14	−0.01
Average wages	0.23	0.07	−0.05	−0.12
Productivity	0.15	0.55*	0.00	−0.07
Profit	−0.08	0.46*	0.10	0.02

Note: Coefficients that are statistically significant at 5% are signalled by *.

with performance variables such as profit and labour productivity the correlation is weakly positive. At a more disaggregated level, correlation coefficients are close to zero.

For the Ellison–Glaeser index, the correlation is positive (but often not statistically significant) with both activity (employment and sales) and performance (productivity and profit) growth rates at the more aggregated level. Again, at the more disaggregated level, no clear pattern emerges.

3.3.2 Graphical analysis

For each sector we show the evolution of the index of concentration (at the département level) and of a certain number of sectoral variables at the national level: employment, value added per employee, mean wage, and share of exports, in percentage of the average in the industrial sectors.[3] The striking conclusion from the analysis of these graphs is the heterogeneity of sectors in terms of the relation between geographical concentration and performances. Let's take a few examples:

- The relative spatial concentration of the clothing industry has increased in the past twenty years (both when using the Gini and the Ellison–Glaeser indices) whereas the share of this sector in industrial employment decreased. However, performances of the sector have improved considerably: the mean wage has increased between 1984 and 2004 from around

---

[3] All variables were smoothed around on a five-year moving average.

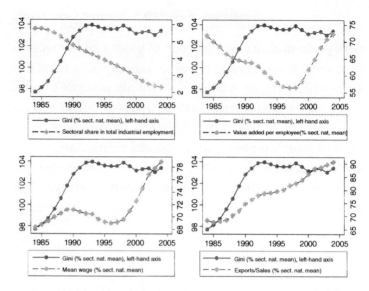

Figure 3.1 Spatial concentration and performance of clothing industry—Gini

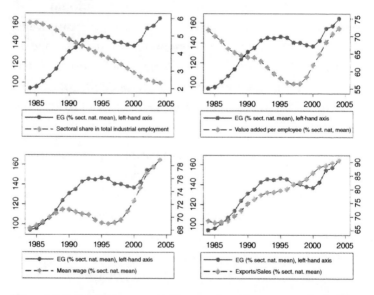

Figure 3.2 Spatial concentration and performance of clothing industry—EG

68 per cent to 78 per cent of the national average. The share of exports in total sales has grown from 65 per cent to 90 per cent of the national mean. Hence, this suggests that the employment losses of the sector have been concentrated in a small number of areas and among the least productive and profitable firms.

- The conclusion is quite different for the metal products sector which has also experienced an increase in its relative geographical concentration during the 1984–2004 period, but a deterioration in its value added per employee, wage, and exports share performances relatively to the national average. Note that on the contrary, the share of the sector in the industrial employment increased over the period.

- The electrical components industry tends to undergo a relative geographical deconcentration whereas its performances in terms of productivity and mean wage per employee tend to increase with respect to other sectors.

- The rubber industry tends to deconcentrate (at least when measured by the Gini index) whereas its relative performances deteriorate over the period.

- For the automobile sector, geographical concentration increases due to sectoral concentration, as the Gini coefficient increases but not the Ellison–Glaeser one. If certain regularities can be detected between the Gini coefficient and the sectoral performances, this is not the case for the Ellison–Glaeser one.

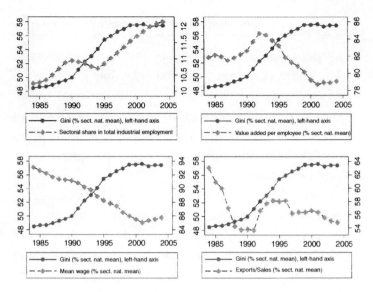

Figure 3.3 Spatial concentration and performance of metal products industry—Gini

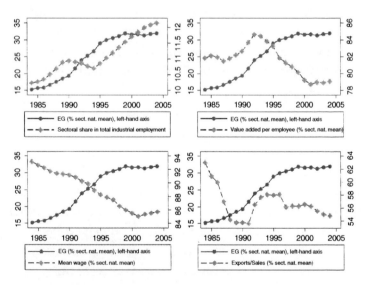

Figure 3.4 Spatial concentration and performance of metal products industry—EG

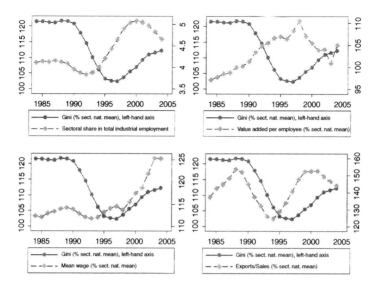

Figure 3.5 Spatial concentration and performance of electrical components industry—Gini

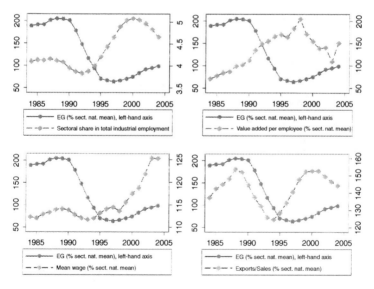

Figure 3.6 Spatial concentration and performance of electrical components industry—EG

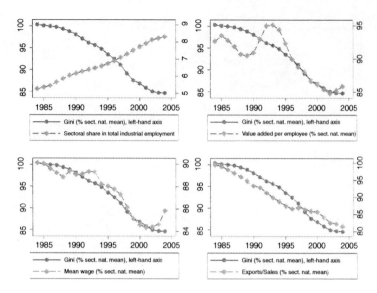

Figure 3.7 Spatial concentration and performance of rubber/tyres industry—Gini

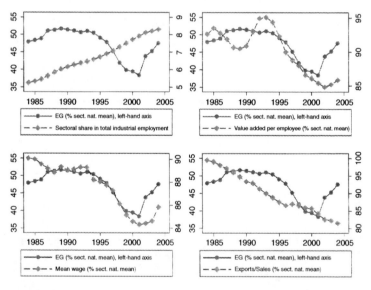

Figure 3.8 Spatial concentration and performance of rubber/tyres industry—EG

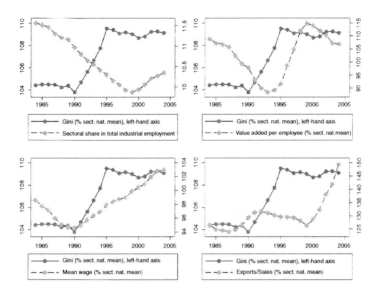

Figure 3.9 Spatial concentration and performance of cars and parts industry—Gini

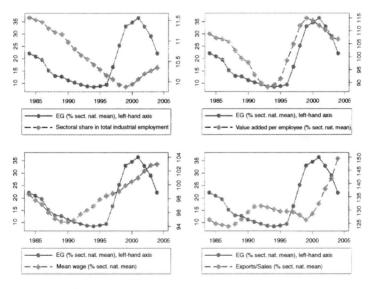

Figure 3.10 Spatial concentration and performance of cars and parts industry—EG

To summarize, there is no uniform pattern across sectors: geographical concentration or dispersion can be associated with very different patterns in terms of performance. This already points to the danger of a public policy that would push uniformly towards more clustering. Not all sectors seem to 'naturally' choose clustering, and clustering is not uniformly associated with better performance. To better understand the potential benefits of clustering, we therefore need a more detailed empirical approach, and in particular a firm-level based approach.

4

Measuring Economic Gains from Clusters

4.1 Does clustering make clusters prosperous?

The chapter on the rationale of clusters showed that cluster policies may have some payoff but their design and implementation are much more complicated than cluster proponents would like us to believe. Furthermore cluster policies can easily be captured by special interests. These concerns may be brushed aside on the grounds that even an imperfect cluster policy could still provide large economic benefits. Thus, it is time to look at the facts regarding the effects of clustering.

4.1.1 *How to measure clusters?*

To estimate the benefits of clustering, two key measurement issues need to be addressed. They regard the industrial and spatial scope of clusters.

The theoretical sections talk of 'activities' without try-ing to be more precise. Porter is equally vague when he talks of 'fields'. Not only is he vague (like many other cluster proponents) but he insists on the idea that 'cluster boundaries rarely conform to standard industrial classifi-cations systems, which fail to capture many important linkages across industries' (Porter 2000b: 18). This point is underscored over and over again in the cluster policy literature. A roughly similar point is made by Porter and his followers about the spatial scope of clusters, which, they argue, do not conform to the boundaries of custom-ary spatial units such as states, counties, or metropolitan areas.

These two points made by cluster proponents are undoubtedly true. We do not expect economic activities to tie in very neatly predetermined industrial and spa-tial categories. Nonetheless, these two points are mostly unimportant when it comes to assessing the effects of clusters. The first reason is that most of the examples that are discussed in the cluster literature actually correspond to narrowly defined industries in regions or metropol-itan areas.[1] These narrowly defined industries seem to

---

[1] Some clusters may span much bigger areas. For instance, cluster propo-nents sometimes want to put the cluster tag on very large areas like the US manufacturing belt or some component of it. Sometimes entire countries are even labelled as 'clusters' (Porter 2000b). This may be a stretch. The main issue is that another theoretical framework putting a lot of emphasis on trade linkages between firms across large distances is needed to think about such 'clusters'. The policy implications of this alternative framework then differ from what we described above. For more on this issue and, more generally, on spatial policies at a larger spatial scale, see Martin (1999), Puga (2002), Ottaviano (2003), and Combes et al. (2005).

be well captured by the standard industrial classifications while their cluster locations are roughly consistent with existing regional and metropolitan boundaries. For instance, the list of the forty-one most important traded clusters in the USA listed in Porter (2003: 565) reads like the North American Industry Classification System: Business Services, Financial Services, Hospitality and Tourism, Education and Knowledge Creation, and Distribution Services, to name only the first five on Porter's list.

The second reason is that assessing the benefits of clustering does not require activities in clusters to coincide exactly with standard industrial categories. It only requires clustered activities to be well proxied by standard industrial categories. To see this, note first that the standard method to assess the benefits of clustering involves regressing some local outcomes by sector, such as output per worker or wages on some measures of local employment in the sector (more on that soon). Provided the measurement error on the latter is uncorrelated with other explanatory variables, a correct estimate will be obtained.[2]

It is also possible to use input–output matrices to control for the sectoral linkages underscored by cluster proponents. This is what Dumais et al. (1997) propose in their work. For US counties and states, they measure the

[2] Although a correlation between cluster size and mis-measurement is conceivable (e.g. standard industrial categories capture cluster employment better in small clusters than in big ones), it is hard to imagine large biases here.

size of the local market that a sector faces by summing the size of all the sectors locally and weighting them by their share of inputs bought from that sector. For instance, leather producers face a large market locally when there are many footwear, apparel, and furniture firms around them. A mirror concept can be defined on the input side. This approach certainly captures Porter's definition of a 'geographically proximate group of inter-connected companies' very well. Arguably, the extensive nature of input–output matrices allows research to capture these linkages more comprehensively than the often arbitrary definitions used by cluster proponents.

Dumais et al. (1997) actually go beyond the notion of input–output linkages since they also construct detailed measures for labour market pooling and technological spillovers at the level of each sector in each area. More specifically, for labour market pooling they use a matrix of occupations by sector. A given sector faces a thick local labour market when it and other sectors that employ a large fraction of their workers in similar occupations are locally large. For technological spillovers, the matrix is constructed from patent citations (using the sector of origin of the cited in each patents sector). Many interesting results emerge from this work. The main ones regard the importance of local labour markets versus technological spillovers and input–output linkages to explain clustering effects and the spatial scale at which they matter. Interestingly, this analysis also shows that the magnitudes of clustering effects are not greatly affected when using these sophisticated measures of agglomeration instead of much cruder ones such as local sectoral employment.

What about the spatial scope of clusters? The fact that clusters do not coincide exactly with existing spatial units is another source of measurement error. The early literature on clustering effect was aware of this problem and a simple solution is to run the same regressions at different spatial scales. Similar magnitudes were typically found for relatively small units such as US counties and relatively big units such as US states. Recent comprehensive evidence by Rosenthal and Strange (2001) suggests some attenuation of clustering when one considers gradually larger units (by moving from zipcodes to US states). Rosenthal and Strange (2003) confirm this attenuation result by estimating agglomeration effects at a very fine spatial scale and allowing for spatial lags. Taken together, these results suggest that it is appropriate to use fairly small units like counties or slightly larger ones like metropolitan areas and that doing so is unlikely to result in big measurement errors.

These results are confirmed by two radically different approaches. First, in their analysis of clustering in UK manufacturing industries, Duranton and Overman (2005) use continuous space so that their results are independent of spatial units. They find that about 50 per cent of industries indeed show some tendency to cluster. Interestingly, clustering usually takes place at short and intermediate distances (i.e. between 0 and 50 kilometres). This suggests that metropolitan areas are the most adequate spatial level at which to examine clustering in the UK. Furthermore, the clustering of industries is most apparent at the four-digit level, suggesting that clustering is best explored using finely defined industries. In further research, Duranton and Overman (2008) also look at the co-localization of industries related through input–output linkages. Consistent with the assertions of cluster proponents, they find that vertically related industries do have a tendency to co-locate. However, this co-location takes place at a larger spatial scale (up to 120 km), suggesting that the regional level might be most appropriate in this case.[3]

Second, a detailed analysis of spatial measurement errors is performed by Briant et al. (2010). They estimate the benefits of agglomeration for France using a number of existing spatial units some of which are purely administrative (e.g. départements) while others were defined by economic principles (e.g. employment areas). They also perform the same exercise for entirely arbitrary units (i.e. squares overlayed on a map). Their main finding is that the estimated effects of agglomeration are only marginally affected by the choice of units. At a given spatial scale, economic, administrative, and purely arbitrary

[3] Overall these findings suggest the existence of a 'two-tier clustering' phenomenon with 'narrow clusters' (narrowly defined industries at small spatial scales) surrounded by 'broad clusters' (related industries at a larger spatial scale). Given the short distances involved in narrow clustering, the latter is likely to be driven by direct interaction between workers (spillovers) and local labour market effects. The broader spatial scale at which vertically linked industries co-localize suggests a more important role for trade linkages to explain broad clustering. This two-tier clustering raises a number of interesting issues regarding cluster policies which seem to be overlooked by cluster proponents.

units of more or less the same sizes imply roughly similar estimates. Consistent with the attenuation result reported above, there are some differences across spatial scales (when using, say, local labour markets vs. regions), although the magnitudes remain close. Interestingly, the estimates are instead more sensitive to the chosen specification. For instance, controlling properly for the skills of the workforce (or not) can have a dramatic effect on the measured benefits of clustering (see below for more on this).

In conclusion, cluster proponents argue that clusters are extremely hard to measure both in terms of industry and geography. Even though it is true that clusters do not neatly coincide with industrial and spatial categories, existing empirical work suggests that the measurement errors made when assessing the benefits of clustering are small when using fine industrial definitions and metropolitan and regional spatial units.[4]

4.1.2 *Cluster productivity benefits exist but are modest*

In this chapter, we deliberately identify the economic gains of clusters to gains from agglomeration externalities. This can be criticized as a narrow view of clusters but it has the great advantage of enabling us to put numbers on a question where impressions dominate.

A large literature attempts to measure various types of agglomeration effects (Rosenthal and Strange 2004).

[4] The interested reader can also refer to the more complete discussion of these issues in Rosenthal and Strange (2004).

A sharp distinction is often made between what is known as 'localization' (i.e. within sectors) and 'urbanization' (i.e. across sectors) effects. Despite the claims of cluster proponents and in light of the discussion above, cluster effects are essentially equivalent to localization effects (or, more precisely, we expect cluster effects to be captured through the estimation of localization effects as they are called in the economic literature).

To assess the effects of clusters, the proper thought experiment is to ask *what would happen to a local outcome should an activity somewhere become larger, all else being equal.* For instance, what is the effect of a larger local pharmaceutical industry on the productivity of its firms or workers?

The large literature on localization effects is supportive of the existence of benefits from clustering. In other words, the existing evidence is consistent with the idea that the productivity curve used in the above theoretical framework is upward sloping.

The first confirmations for the existence of clustering effects date back to Shefer (1973) and Sveikauskas (1975). For a subset of cities and sectors, Shefer (1973) found that a doubling of local employment in a sector would increase its productivity by up to 25 per cent. Using a more robust approach, Sveikauskas (1975) found much smaller numbers, around 6 to 7 per cent. The subsequent thirty years of research have found numbers very much in line with those of Sveikauskas (1975). More generally, the range of estimates for the mean elasticity of labour productivity to local industry employment is between 2 and 10 per cent with a mid-point around 4 or 5 per cent (Rosenthal and Strange 2004).[5] Put differently, doubling the specialization in a typical activity and area is associated with an increase in productivity of around 4 per cent. This number is lower in some industries and higher in others (although it seldom goes above 10 per cent). Even for industries with strong clustering effects, say, an elasticity of 8 per cent, it takes more than a trebling of the specialization of the cluster to see labour productivity increase by 10 per cent. In conclusion, there are positive effects of clustering but the literature is also strongly suggestive that it takes extremely large increases in specialization to get more than marginal effects on local productivity and wages.

Even though the effects estimated by the literature are modest, they probably exaggerate the true (i.e. causal) benefits of clustering on productivity. First, many studies do not estimate a 'pure' effect of clustering (i.e. an increase in specialization keeping total employment constant). Instead, these studies assess the effect of an increase in the size of the industry of employment, keeping employment in all other industries constant. Doing so conflates the effect of increased clustering with the effect of being in an area with more employment overall (since increasing the size of one industry keeping all other industries equal means an overall increase in

---

[5] For the sake of brevity only the coefficient on local employment is discussed. Many studies try to capture the effects of clustering through the local number of firms and other measures of local industry 'size' as well as employment. Doing this does not affect the conclusions reported here.

employment). The second effect is arguably an 'urban growth' effect (or urbanization effect) and not a cluster effect. Since this growth effect may be independent of the sector of employment, it should not be counted as part of clustering. This (arcane) distinction matters a lot here because urbanization effects tend to be quite large, whereas cluster proponents do not argue in favour of growth in general but only for the development of specific activities.

Furthermore, most studies in the literature fail to control for the fact that causation may not run from clustering to high local productivity and wages but instead from the latter to the former.[6] If causation were to go in the opposite direction, i.e. from high productivity to high employment, all the results in the literature prior to the mid-1990s would be biased upward and thus exaggerate the magnitude of clustering effects.

Most agglomerated areas might be areas with better endowments (public infrastructure, climate, etc.). For example, wine is produced in California because the climate is better there than in Minnesota. Moreover, Baldwin and Okubo (2006), marrying Melitz and Otta-viano (2008)'s approach with a New Economic Geography model, show that a selection process may be at work in denser areas: most productive firms sell more and are consequently more likely to gain from backward

[6] Even when the mobility of the workforce is very low, substantial movements of workers can occur in the long run. Going back to an example used above, the Californian wine production cluster may be bigger than that of upstate New York because the returns on wine-making are intrinsically higher in California.

and forward linkages in clusters than the others; they are also more likely to resist the tougher competition or the higher price of land in denser areas. There could consequently be reverse causality and selection bias: firms cluster in some territories because of the better amenities of those territories, and only the most productive firms can sustain the clustering process.

Moreover, the increase (or decrease) of local employment may be, at least partly, due to conjunctural effects which also impact on firms' performance. If there is a positive demand shock, the total factor productivity of firms (or workers' productivity) and the number of producing firms (or of workers employed by those firms) will both increase. There would be apparently a cluster effect whereas it is in fact only due to a conjunctural effect: that is the simultaneity bias. Researchers must account for those pitfalls carefully in order to highlight a real causal relationship between clusters and productivity.

The first analysis that tackled this reverse-causation issue head-on was Ciccone and Hall (1996). Determining the direction of causation is one of the hardest endeavours in applied economics. To do this, one needs to find some exogenous determinants of the variable that is suspected of endogeneity (e.g. local employment). The key restriction is that these exogenous determinants (or instruments) should be correlated with the variable to be explained (e.g. local productivity or local wages) only through the endogenous variable. Finding such determinants of local employment that are otherwise uncorrelated with local wealth is hard. For the USA, Ciccone and Hall (1996) propose a number of them, which are related to the patterns of settlement of that country. Among others, they use the presence of early railroads in a county or its distance from the eastern seaboard. They found that there was no large endogeneity bias when estimating agglomeration effects at the level of US states (wherein counties are aggregated in a particular way).

Using a different set of instruments and conducting their analysis at the level of smaller areas (French local labour markets instead of US states), Combes et al. (2008) find evidence of some reverse causation. These findings are consistent with those of Ciccone and Hall (1996) since reverse causation is much more likely at a small spatial scale. This is because short-distance moves (or even adjustments in commuting patterns) are less costly than long-distance moves. Overall, the prevailing conclusion at this stage is that reverse causation probably biases existing estimates upwards, but only mildly so (Rosenthal and Strange 2004).

An alternative approach to circumvent the possible simultaneous determination of clustering and wages or productivity is to use firm panel data as in Henderson (2003). His work is actually the closest to the approach we adopted in that book. His data are available at five-year intervals from 1972 to 1992. He estimates a plant-level production function for two broad sectors, machinery industries and high-tech industries, and measures the elasticity of total factor productivity to the number of other plants of the same industry in the county. Using industry-time and plant/location fixed effects, he finds a positive and significant elasticity of 8 per cent in the high-tech industry only. He does not find evidence of urbanization economies. The use of fixed effects accounts for a large part of unobserved heterogeneity. Henderson also addresses the question of simultaneity bias by adding location-time fixed effects.

A last concern with respect to the proper estimation of localization effects is that the skills of workers need to be properly controlled for.[7] The estimates are biased upwards again when better workers in the industry work in larger clusters. Arguably the most productive workers in the UK finance industry will be employed in London, its largest cluster. Those working in secondary financial centres such as Leeds are likely to be less productive. Finally those working where the industry is very small are likely to be even less productive, etc. Failing to control properly for skills will lead to the wrong attribution of the effects of greater skills to cluster size and thus bias the results. Controlling properly for skills is hard because many dimensions of skills are unobserved by the statistician. Using the longitudinal dimension of their data for French workers, Combes et al. (2008) find this bias to be relatively large. The estimated elasticity of wages to specialization drops from a cross-sector average

---

[7] An alternative concern is that these differences in wages may only reflect difference in hours worked. Better studies control for this and show that this is not the case. It is nonetheless interesting to know that workers in professional occupations, and especially the young ones, work more hours in larger cities while workers in other occupations tend to work fewer hours than in smaller cities (Rosenthal and Strange 2008). However, the effects are rather small.

of 4.3 per cent to 2.1 per cent when controlling for observed and unobserved skills. This suggests that the standard estimates of specialization elasticities in the literature may need to be divided by two. If these low numbers were confirmed, cluster specialization would need to become very high to obtain a non-trivial increase in labour productivity.

Even more negative conclusions are obtained by de Blasio and Di Addario (2005). Their study is of particular interest because they perform their analysis on Italian spatial units that were explicitly defined using a cluster mapping project. They do not find any positive evidence of a wage premium for workers in clusters. Their findings are even suggestive of lower returns to education in clusters! These results may be specific to Italian clusters (which would be ironic given the attention that Italian clusters have received in the literature). However, this lack of cluster effect is more likely to be caused by a subtle but interesting methodological difference. In their work, de Blasio and Di Addario (2005) attempt to assess the wage effect of working in a cluster regardless of the industry of employment, whereas the rest of the literature looks at the effect of an increase in specialization on the wages of workers in the same industry. There may be no contradiction between the two sets of results. The literature finds positive cluster effects for workers employed in the main sector of the cluster, while de Blasio and Di Addario (2005) fail to find evidence of broader benefits that would accrue to all workers.

At this stage, it is fair to conclude that there are modest positive effects of clustering on labour productivity and wages. They appear to benefit only workers in the same sector of employment. There is still an open debate about whether these effects are small or very small, but the evidence presented here is certainly not supportive of large positive economic returns associated with cluster development. Nonetheless, the fact that *returns* to clustering are small may not run against the idea that clustering can make an important *contribution* to local productivity and local wages. It is not because a coefficient is small that the contribution to an outcome associated with its variable is necessarily small. Unfortunately, assessing the contribution of clustering to high local wages or high local productivity is not an exercise that is often performed in the economic literature.

Combes et al. (2008) are an exception. They report detailed results regarding the contribution of a range of local industry variables to individual wages. Their first result is that even when they are considered together, clustering variables (specialization, number of local industry establishments, local share of industry professionals, etc.) only make a very small contribution to local wages. More formally, the partial R^2 of the clustering variables in regressions purporting to explain individual wages are very low. This partial R^2 is, for instance, much smaller than that of other variables included in the regression such as labour market experience. In conclusion, the effects of clustering on wages and labour productivity are small and the overall contribution of clustering to wages and productivity is even smaller.

4.1.3 *The channels through which clustering benefits clusters*

It would also be important to understand where those clustering and agglomeration effects are coming from. Put differently, through which channel does clustering improve productivity? Knowing the answer to this would obviously be of prime importance for the proper design of cluster policies. Unfortunately, the literature on this issue does not provide very strong conclusions. Identifying the channels through which clustering effects percolate is extremely difficult. The reason behind this is that many clustering mechanisms share the same predictions regarding productivity outcomes.

A first solution is to use proxies for the various sources of benefits from clustering. Building on Dumais et al. (1997), this is what Rigby and Essletzbichler (2002) do. Their results show that local labour pooling plays a prominent role together with input–output linkages in determining agglomeration benefits. This is consistent with the more indirect findings of Dumais et al. (1997), Rosenthal and Strange (2001), and Ellison et al. (2010). Nonetheless, some care is needed in the interpretation of these results due to significant econometric and data challenges. First, a stronger association between clustering benefits and an 'adequate' local labour market is obviously consistent with a causal link running from the latter to the former. However, the composition of the local labour market and high cluster benefits could be simultaneously determined. For instance, Silicon Valley's labour market may contain the exact right mix of workers but this may be a consequence (and not a cause) of a very successful cluster with costs of living so high that only those who stand to gain the most stay there. Second, the proxies used to measure labour market pooling may be much better than those used to measure technological spillovers (for which the paper trails are extremely scarce). Since those proxies are likely to be highly correlated, most of the correlation with clustering benefits may be sucked up by the better proxies regardless of the role that they actually play in clustering.

For some particular mechanisms research has been able to circumvent these data limitations and identification issues by focusing very narrowly on one specific mechanism and ignoring the others. For instance, Jaffe et al. (1993) attempt to get at the issue of local spillovers by examining geographical biases in patent citations. They ask whether patents developed nearby have a greater chance of being cited than patents developed further away, all else being equal. Their initial results hinted at a substantial bias whereby patents originating from the same metropolitan areas are nearly three times as likely to be cited as patents from other metropolitan areas. Despite a very high level of care in the data work, subsequent research has disputed these findings and the current wisdom is that the bias is possibly no higher than 25 per cent and short-lived, as knowledge may diffuse nationally quite rapidly (Thompson 2006). In a very different vein, Holmes (1999) shows that clustered firms are more likely to out-source and buy their inputs locally, etc.

This type of work is important because it explores specific mechanisms and unique predictions of particular clustering stories. However, it only provides an 'existence proof' about these mechanisms and no magnitude regarding their importance. Recent work has tried to map this type of approach into a productivity framework. Using workplace communication data at the level of individual workers, Charlot and Duranton (2004) find that up to 20 per cent of the benefits from clustering percolate through workplace communication. Given the difficulty of finding the right data and the econometric challenges associated with this type of exercise, progress on the identification of the sources of clustering benefits can only be slow and tentative. Unfortunately detailed cluster policies will require knowing what matters to determine clustering benefits and where the inefficiencies are.

The work on the dynamic effects of clustering is largely inspired by theories on endogenous growth (Romer 1986; Lucas 1988). The idea is that geographical agglomeration does not only favour productivity but also productivity growth at firm level. Consequently, at local level, the more an area is specialized in a given industry, the higher is productivity growth of that industry in that area. But researchers were confronted by a lack of reliable data on firms' and regions' productivity, whereas data on local employment by industries were available. Therefore, a crucial assumption is made in most studies on dynamic externalities: productivity growth is supposed to imply employment growth. Consequently, whereas the theory invites us to assess the impact of geographic agglomeration of activities on firms' productivity, Glaeser et al. (1992), Henderson et al. (1995), or Combes (2000) examine the effect of specialization and of industrial diversity on local employment growth.

Glaeser et al. (1992) find, on American data, that sectoral employment growth at local level is negatively affected by specialization. On the contrary, industrial diversity seems to favour sectoral employment growth. Combes (2000) also finds a rather negative impact of specialization on employment growth in both industry and services in France, but his results tend to show that industrial diversity enhances employment growth in services only. Henderson et al. (1995) show on American data that mature industries tend to be subject to localization economies, but not to urbanization externalities, whereas high-tech industries are subject to both economies.

Therefore, most studies based on employment growth do not confirm the existence of positive dynamic externalities from specialization, and even tend to show a negative impact of specialization on local sectoral employment growth, whereas evidence about dynamic urbanization economies is rather mixed.

Nevertheless, Cingano and Schivardi (2004) cast serious doubt on those results. Indeed, the assumption that productivity growth implies employment growth is not valid, for example, if the demand for the good is too inelastic. Localization economies might enhance productivity and reduce local employment at the same time. The authors confirm this intuition studying the Italian case. They use firm-level data to construct indices of Total Factor Productivity at industry and Local Labor Systems[8] level. They regress TFP growth at industry and LLS level between 1986 and 1998 on variables of local specialization, diversity, city size, firm size, competition, etc. in 1986. They find a positive and significant impact of specialization and city size, but no effect of diversity and competition. An interesting finding is that the same regression realized on local sectoral employment growth rate gives results very similar to Combes's or Glaeser et al.'s ones: specialization and city size negatively affect local employment growth, whereas sectoral diversity has a positive impact. Consequently, the conclusions about agglomeration economies based on the local sectoral employment growth approach appear spurious, due to a specification problem.

Since estimating productivity growth is fraught with difficulties, an alternative way to assess the dynamic benefits from clustering would be to look at a range of other outcomes to get at the productivity effects of clustering indirectly. Innovation is usually singled out by cluster proponents (Porter 2000b, 2003).[9] The literature

---

[8] Defined on the basis of workers' commuting.

[9] This fascination with innovation may not be warranted. At the aggregate level, a good argument can be made that innovation and welfare are

on agglomeration effects with respect to innovation is much smaller than that looking at productivity outcomes. Nonetheless, the findings are generally not supportive of strong clustering effects on innovation (Duranton and Puga 2000). On the contrary, Feldman and Audretsch (1999), in a leading study, report that local innovation is fostered by a more diverse production structure. Local specialization has instead a sizeable negative effect on innovation.

In conclusion, clustering offers small 'static' productivity benefits and there is no strong evidence of positive dynamic (or innovation) benefits. Put differently, the literature that attempts to assess the effects of clustering only offers very weak support to the claims made by cluster proponents. We are now ready to give further evidence on economic gains of clusters based on the French experience.

4.2 Methodology to assess the causal impact of agglomeration

We quantify the impact of both clustering effects (or intra-sectoral localization effects) economies and urbanization (inter-sectoral) economies on total factor productivity (TFP) of French firms. The results presented in this chapter are part of a more technical work by Martin et al. (2008a).

strongly linked. The link between local innovation and local welfare could possibly be much more tenuous and should be scrutinized further.

To clarify our approach, we use a standard Cobb–Douglas production function which relates the value added of firms to their TFP, their capital stock, and their labour force (the number of employees). The objective is to quantify the impact of localization and urbanization economies on the TFP of the firms, that is on the value added of the firm once its factors of production (capital and labour) have been taken into account. The production function (all in log terms) is then:

$$y_{it} = \alpha k_{it} + \beta l_{it} + \delta \text{cluster}_{it}^{sz} + \gamma \text{urb}_{it}^{sz} + u_{it}, \qquad (4.1)$$

where y_{it} is the value added, observed for all firms over time in our data, k_{it} the capital stock, and l_{it} the labour force of firm i at time t. We then assume that TFP of i depends upon a firm-level component, u_{it}, but also on its immediate environment: cluster_{it}^{sz} is an index of clustering economies and urb_{it}^{sz} is an index of urbanization economies for firm i, which belongs to sector s and area z, at time t. The model can be estimated by a simple ordinary least squares (OLS) regression if all the independent variables are observable and at least weakly exogenous, but that hypothesis is rarely respected.

It is not straightforward to establish causality in the statistical relationship between agglomeration and productivity. This type of regression suffers from two main sources of endogeneity: (i) unobserved heterogeneity in the attractiveness of locations and (ii) simultaneity bias. Most agglomerated areas might be areas with better endowments (public infrastructure, climate, etc.) or may attract more productive firms for various reasons.

One of those could be related to localized public policy. Wise, but unobserved, decisions made by local authorities could lead to a higher local productivity, which attracts firms and therefore leads to the false impression that spatial concentration of firms per se spurs higher productivity. There is therefore the risk that agglomeration economies are overestimated if this unobserved heterogeneity is not taken into account. One way to deal with this issue is to introduce a relevant set of fixed effects, which will absorb all time-invariant sources of unobserved heterogeneity.

However, an additional simultaneity problem might be at work in this type of estimation. It cannot be dealt with through the use of fixed effects. The increase (or decrease) of local employment may be, at least partly, due to cyclical effects which also impact on firms' performance; this simultaneity issue could also bias the results.

A further issue is the inadequacy of the data used in many empirical studies to measure directly agglomeration externalities. Indeed, the theories which underlie those externalities are microeconomic in essence. Consequently, their empirical validity is best verified with firm-level data. In the absence of such data, many studies have tried to measure indirectly agglomeration externalities, using more aggregated data on sectoral employment at local level. While this issue is different from the endogeneity problem, it contributes to strengthen it, since the omitted variable bias or reverse causality issues mentioned above have all chances to be more severe when using local aggregate levels of wages or productivity as a dependent variable.

The use of firm-level panel data allows us to reduce a great deal those endogeneity concerns, through the greater detail of the dependent variable, which can be combined with the use of firm or plant fixed effects. If the time span of our sample is rather short (which is the case here, 1996–2004), we can be quite confident that the stability of unobservables taken into account by fixed effects is not a big issue here. A further point is that unobserved heterogeneity is not the only source of endogeneity affecting agglomeration effects estimation. Consequently, we will resort to an instrumentation strategy to resolve the simultaneity problem and, in doing so, we will also correct for possible remaining unobservables.

To address the simultaneity issue, a possible approach is to follow recent dynamic panel data approaches. Start by taking first differences of each variable, to address the unobserved heterogenity issue. Then instrument the first-differenced independent variables by their level at time $t-2$. The underlying econometric assumption is that the idiosyncratic shock at time $t-2$ is orthogonal to the difference of the error terms in t and $t-1$. Under this assumption, the instruments are exogenous, which solves our problem. Sargan-Hansen of joint validity of instruments can be used to test this hypothesis.

A drawback of this approach is the focus on first differences, which might be problematic if agglomeration economies come from technological/knowledge spillovers, which might take more time to fully enter into action. However, labour market or input-related external-ities might be faster. The economic rationale for the use of lagged levels of variables to instrument their first differences is convergence: for each variable, we expect first differences to be negatively correlated to the past level of variables. Bigger firms are expected to have a lower growth rate of the number of employees and capital and so on for all variables. First-stage regressions can be used to validate this idea.

To summarize, while the statistical inference of a causal relationship between productivity and agglomeration is a very challenging task with no definitive solution, the combination of firm-level data availability with modern panel data techniques can go a long way to neutralize the most obvious sources of endogeneity.

4.3 Data and variables

We present here the data we use, the way we build our sample, and some issues about the construction of our variables.

4.3.1 *The French annual business survey*

We use French annual business survey[10] data, provided by the French Ministry of Industry. We have information at firm and plant level. They cover firms with more than

---

[10] Called in French 'Enquêtes annuelles d'entreprises'.

twenty employees and all the plants of those firms. Our data cover the 1996–2004 period.

At the firm level, we have all balance-sheet data (production, value added, employment, capital, exports, aggregate wages, etc.) and information about firm location, firm industry classification, and firm structure (number of plants etc.). At the plant level, data are less precise; they mainly contain plant location, plant industry classification, number of employees, and information about the firm the plant belongs to.

4.3.2 *The variables*

Firm value added, employees, and capital (measured at the beginning of the year) are directly available in the annual business surveys. The creation of agglomeration variables is more elaborate. First of all, the geographical and the sectoral level of aggregation could have an impact on our measure of clustering effects.[11] This is why we decided to focus on two geographical entities, the départements, which are administrative entities (there are 100 départements in France, of which 4 are overseas départements) and the employment areas, which are economic entities defined on the basis of workers' commuting (there are 348 employment areas in metropolitan France). From a sectoral point of view, we consider the French activities classification (Naf) at both

[11] For more details about the impact of spatial zoning on economic geography estimations, see Briant et al. (2010).

the three- and two-digit levels. Consequently, we create our agglomeration variables at four levels: employment area/Naf 3-digit, employment area/Naf 2-digit, département/Naf 3-digit, and département/Naf 2-digit. The definition of our variables follows:

- *clustering effects*: to deal with intra-industry externalities, we measure, for each firm, the number of other employees working in the same industry and in the same area. Concretely, we use the annual business surveys at plant level and calculate the number of workers by year, industry, and area. For firm i, in industry s, in area z at time t, we then define our clustering effect variable as:

$$\text{cluster}_{it}^{sz} = \ln(\text{employees}_t^{sz} - \text{employees}_{it}^{sz} + 1)$$

At that stage, two remarks are in order. First, ideally, we should estimate a production function at plant level. But capital data are only available at the firm level, which is a problem for multi-plant firms. Rather than making strong assumptions on the distribution of capital among plants, we run our estimations at the firm level; we use for agglomeration variables the values relative to the area where the firm's headquarter is registered. However, a firm can have several plants in different départements or employment areas, so that it can declare a number of employees greater than the number of workers in the industry on its territory of registration; in other words, $\text{employees}_t^{sz} - \text{employees}_{it}^{sz}$ is possibly

113

negative. In that case, we drop the observation. To check that the presence of multi-plant firms does not bias our results, we also run the estimations on a sample of single-plant firms; the results remain very similar.

- *urbanization economies*: we use two variables to capture urbanization economies. The first one is the number of workers in the other industries on the territory z where firm i is located. Hence, with the same notation, we have:

$$\text{urb}_t^{sz} = \ln(\text{employees}_t^z - \text{employees}_t^{sz} + 1)$$

We also add an Herfindahl index of diversity, defined as follows:

$$H_t^{sz} = \sum_{j \neq s} [\text{employees}_{jt}^z / (\text{employees}_t^z - \text{employees}_t^{sz})]^2$$

The index $\text{div}_t^{sz} = 1/H_{szt}$ will be an indicator of the diversity that firms of industry s face on territory z at time t.

Finally, we introduce a variable controlling for local strength of competition. The use of such a variable aims at verifying Porter's idea about competition and agglomeration: local competition stirs innovation so that more intense competition within clusters improves firms' performance (Porter 1998a). We therefore use an Herfindahl index of industrial concentration:

$$\text{Herf}_t^{sz} = \sum_{i \in S_t^z} (\text{employees}_{it}^{sz} / \text{employees}_t^{sz})^2$$

where S_t^z is the set of firms belonging to industry s on territory z at time t.[12] The variable $\text{comp}_t^{sz} = 1/\text{Herf}_t^{sz}$ measures the degree of competition a firm of sector s faces on territory z at time t. Which brings us to the relationship we want to bring to data:

$$y_{it} = \alpha k_{it} + \beta l_{it} + \delta \text{loc}_{it}^{sz} + \gamma \text{urb}_{it}^{sz} + \mu \text{div}_t^{sz} + \lambda \text{comp}_t^{sz} + \phi_i + \epsilon_{it}.$$
$$(4.2)$$

4.3.3 Construction of the sample

We create four samples, crossing the two territorial levels (départements and employment areas) and the two sectoral classifications (Naf 3-digit and Naf 2-digit) we are interested in.

From a geographical point of view, we drop all firms located in Corsica and in overseas départements. Consequently, our samples cover the 94 and the 341 continental French départements and employment areas. Industry-wise, we keep in the sample firms belonging to manufacturing sectors only.[13]

For each sample, we drop all firms which changed geographical unit or industrial sector during the period.

---

[12] We constructed Herf_t^{sz} from plant-level data, so that $employees_{iszt}$ is really the number of employees working in plants of firm i on territory z at time t.

[13] In the French 2-digit classification, manufacturing sectors correspond to sectors 16 to 36. In particular, food-processing firms have been dropped, since the information related to those comes from a different survey, not entirely compatible with the rest of manufacturing. In the end, the sample spans over twenty 2-digit and ninety 3-digit industrial sectors.

We also made basic error checks; among other things, we dropped all observations for which value added, employment, or capital was missing, negative, or null. We deflated value added data by an industry-level price index and capital data by a national investment price index.

Finally we cleaned up our sample from large outliers, dropping the 1 per cent extreme values for the following variables: average labour productivity, capital intensity, yearly capital growth rate, yearly employment growth rate, yearly average labour productivity growth rate, yearly average capital intensity growth rate.

4.3.4 *Summary statistics*

We show here the summary statistics at the employment area/Naf 3-digit level. But in all the four samples,

Table 4.1 Temporal composition of the sample Naf 3-digit/employment area sample

Year	Observations	%	Cum. %
1996	16110	12.2	12.2
1997	15136	11.46	23.66
1998	14946	11.32	34.97
1999	14850	11.24	46.21
2000	14549	11.01	57.23
2001	14579	11.04	68.26
2002	14351	10.86	79.13
2003	14023	10.62	89.75
2004	13545	10.25	100.00
Total	132089	100.00	

Table 4.2 Summary statistics Naf 3-digit/employment area

Variable	Observations	Mean	Std. dev.	Min	Max
Value added	132089	4221.29	13538.30	32.39	1236850
Firm's employment	132089	90.92	196.68	1	16734
Firm's capital	132089	4441.57	17379.50	6.66	2077673
Firm's capital intensity	132089	35.47	35.47	0.80	273.12
Firm's labour productivity	132089	41.30	19.63	11.71	164.31
No. employees, other firms, same industry area	132089	1290.75	3172.79	0	24508
No. other firms, same industry area	132089	22.87	59.98	0	522
No. employees, other industries, same area	132089	27910.17	32689.73	18	146517
No. firms, other industries, same area	132089	380.05	480.08	5	2321

Note: Value-added, capital, capital intensity, and labour productivity are expressed in thousands of real euros.

statistics are not very different, except for the fact that, as expected, clustering effect variables are bigger when measured at the level of the département rather than at the employment area level (this is also true for urbanization variables), and at the Naf 2-digit level rather than at the Naf 3-digit level (whereas urbanization variables are bigger at the Naf 3-digit level).

We can see in Table 4.1 that the size of our sample decreases over the period. This is due to the de-industrialization phenomenon that France, like many other developed countries, has been undergoing in the last decades.

Table 4.2 shows the usual descriptive statistics of our variables. First note that most variables exhibit strong variability, as shown by the large values of standard deviations respective to their mean.

As our data sources mainly cover firms with more than twenty employees, the average size of the firms of our sample is quite large (ninety employees). The minimum value for the cluster measure (in terms of employees and of firms) is zero: some firms are the only representative of their industry in their employment area. For those firms, there are consequently no clustering effects.[14]

---

[14] Since $\text{cluster}_{it}^{sz} = \ln(\text{employees}_t^{sz} - \text{employees}_{it}^{sz} + 1)$, $\text{cluster}_{it}^{sz} = 0$ when $\text{employees}_t^{sz} - \text{employees}_{it}^{sz} = 0$.

4.4 The strength of agglomeration economies

4.4.1 Which type of agglomeration economies?

Our results are clear and non-ambiguous: French firms benefit from clustering effects but not from being in an economically diverse territory. This conclusion does not depend on the sectoral or the geographical level we consider.

We mentioned two main sources of biases when estimating clustering effects: denser areas may be areas with better endowments, and denser areas may attract the most productive firms (Baldwin and Okubo effect). Both effects are corroborated by our results (see Martin et al. 2008a). They suggest that places with better endowments attract firms from all industries, and that better infrastructures improve the productivity of firms. Our results also suggest that high-productivity firms locate in the territories with a high level of competition.

When we control for the selection bias and for the problem of simultaneity,[15] only the clustering effect remains significant. For a firm, all else being equal, a doubling of the number of employees of its own 3-digit industry in the employment area would increase its productivity by 4.9 per cent.[16] We do not find evidence

[15] We use a regression with first-differenced variables, instrumented by their level at time $t - 2$. See Martin et al. (2008a) for the full results.

[16] Strictly speaking, the number is actually lower. The elasticity of TFP to clustering is 0.049 so that a 1% increase in clustering leads to a 0.049% increase in TFP: $(1.01)^{0.049} = 1.00049$. But to compute a large increase such as a 100% increase, the approximation is not right and the true impact is: $2^{0.049} = 1.0345$ a 3.45% increase in productivity.

of urbanization economies à la Jacobs nor evidence of competition effect à la Porter. This result is qualitatively the same for any level of geographical and/or industrial aggregation. However, the coefficient on the clustering effect varies from 4.9 per cent to 13.8 per cent according to the chosen aggregation level. It is interesting to note that, in spite of methodological differences, our results are qualitatively and quantitatively very similar to what has been measured on Italian or American data (see Cingano and Schivardi 2004 and Henderson 2003).

4.4.2 Is the impact of localization economies large?

In our sample, for a firm, the average growth rate of the number of employees, same 3-digit industry/same employment area, is 5.5 per cent: at that pace, it takes almost thirteen years to double the size of an industry to which a firm belongs to in the employment area it is located in. Each year, only 50 per cent of the firms undergo an increase of their potential for clustering effects. Over the period, only 2.5 per cent of the firms experienced a change of the size of their industry around them larger than a doubling. This means that at the firm level, the doubling of the number of employees (of the same industry and same location) that we found was necessary to increase TFP by 4.9 per cent is actually a very rare event. It naturally raises the question whether a public policy can easily generate such a change in local economic geography.

We can also ask the question on the size of the clustering effect in another way: how much does this effect explain the difference in the value added across French firms? To answer this question, we computed the variation of value added induced by a standard deviation of the three determinants: the two factors of production (capital and labour) and the clustering effect. We calculated the explanatory power of employees, capital, and of the clustering effect at each level of industrial and geographic aggregation we retained in the construction of our samples (see section 4.3.3).

Table 4.3 shows that clustering effects are of second order relative to capital and labour to explain the value added. However, they are not negligible as they explain between 9.3 per cent and 17.6 per cent of the difference in value added between French firms. Note that the effect is much larger at the Naf 2-digit level than at the Naf 3-digit level, and a slightly bigger variation at the département level than at the employment area level. Those differences can however be a statistical artefact (see Briant et al. 2010 on this question). The difference induced by the choice of industrial nomenclature may be due to the fact that clustering effect occurs in a broader field than the quite narrow definition of 3-digit sectors (ninety sectors in our samples). The Naf 2-digit nomenclature (twenty sectors in our samples) would consequently better capture the whole set of positive

Table 4.3 Explanatory power of main variables (%)

Variable	Employment area/ Naf 3-digit	Département/ Naf 3-digit	Employment area/ Naf 2-digit	Département/ Naf 2-digit
Employees	64.5	74.7	72.8	75.2
Capital	29.9	28.8	34.2	32.1
No. employees, other firms, same industry-area	9.3	10.5	16.8	17.6

Note: The table reads as follows: for a firm, all other things being equal, a standard deviation of the number of own employees generates, in the Naf 3-digit/Employment area regression, an increase of value added of 64.5%.

externalities induced by the agglomeration of activities, such as vertical linkages for example.

At this point, we can therefore conclude that the starting point of cluster policies is right: there are positive and significant effects of the clustering effect of activities. But these effects, while not negligible, are not very large and certainly no miracle can be expected from a reasonably realistic change in economic geography.

4.5 Additional issues on localization economies

4.5.1 Employees, firms, or plants externalities?

We have defined so far the clustering effect for an industry in terms of employees. However, one could argue that the positive externalities from clustering come from a large number of firms rather than from a larger number of employees. For a firm, does it matter whether the cluster around it is made of one firm with a hundred employees or ten firms, each of them employing ten workers? The question may be of interest for policy makers who want to implement a cluster policy; according to the answer, the cluster policy should aim to increase either the size of existing firms or the number of firms located in the cluster.

Henderson (2003) finds that plants generate externalities, but not workers. If we consider each plant as a source of knowledge, this result is the sign, according to Henderson, that information spillovers are more important than labour market externalities.

Our results are different. We introduced in the regressions the clustering and diversity variables expressed in terms of firms, in addition to the ones in terms of employees used until now. We did the same thing with the agglomeration variables expressed in terms of plants. In both cases, only the number of employees is significant. It is noteworthy that when we do not account for the level of sectoral competition at local level, both employees and firms (or plants) are significant. Our results suggest that the effect of the number of firms (plants) passes through some kind of competition effect. Since Henderson does not control for competition, this could be an explanation for our apparently contradictory results.

To sum up, the case of French firms indicates that there are no specific externalities we can attribute to firms per se but that there are positive and significant externalities linked to the number of employees in surrounding firms. The number of employees in the other firms is a better indicator of the size of the industry a firm faces on its territory than the number of firms. This points to an interpretation under which localization economies are, for a firm, due to the 'thickness' of the industry around it. Our results suggest that boosting externalities within clusters involves the promotion of internal growth of existing firms or the attraction of big firms on the territory rather than multiplying the number of small firms. Moreover, our results indicate that externalities linked to the market of inputs and to the creation of a specialized pool of labour (more directly connected to the thickness of the industry than to the number of firms) are potentially important channels of localization economies. That would support the results of Ellison et al. (2010), who find, based on American data, that input–output linkages and labour pooling are—in this order—the two main determinants of industries' co-agglomeration. They also find evidence of knowledge spillovers, but to a lesser degree.

4.5.2 *Localization economies and distance*

What is the geographic scope of localization economies? Assessing the geographic scope of benefits from clustering is an important question for public policy makers in order to define the geographic perimeter of their action. Different approaches have been used in the literature to measure the geographic scope of localization economies or agglomeration patterns: discrete ones, based on political boundaries (such as Henderson 2003), or continuous ones (such as Duranton and Overman 2008).[17]

The existing literature suggests that the benefits from clustering are very localized. According to Henderson (2003), once industrial thickness in the county is taken into account, the number of the industry's plants has no further impact. Duranton and Overman (2008) find that localization patterns of industries in the UK take place within a small perimeter. We address this question on our French data set, using two alternative

---

[17] For a detailed survey, see Rosenthal and Strange (2004).

methods: controlling for the thickness of the industry in the employment area (or département) of the firm, we analyse the influence of contiguous areas on the one hand, and of all the other areas, each of them weighted by its distance from the area of the firm, on the other hand. The only variable to affect significantly the productivity of the firm is the thickness of its sector in its own employment area or département.

Consequently, our results on French data show that cluster benefits are very localized. It is consistent with the literature on spatial scope of knowledge spillovers (see for example Jaffe et al. 1993). This would also support the idea that beyond geographical proximity, organizational proximity and social interactions are probably very important: externalities probably channel through 'high-quality' individual and business relationships. Geographic proximity is necessary to facilitate mutual knowledge and social interactions. This result is interesting for policy makers since it points to the benefits of a very local approach to cluster policies. The recently created French competitiveness clusters take a different approach as they link firms in different employment areas, different départements, and even, for some, different regions.

4.5.3 *Agglomeration and knowledge spillovers*

According to Alfred Marshall, one of the sources of externalities within clusters is knowledge spillovers:

geographic proximity facilitates communication between firms and the diffusion of information among firms increases their productivity. One way to interpret knowledge spillovers is that they come from technological transfers. These transfers of technology should however not be thought of as natural given that these firms are competitors in a given sector. Those transfers are not impossible, but they probably work through formalized cooperations and collaborative projects, far from the famous 'cafeteria effects', which refer to informal social discussions between entrepreneurs or employees of different firms.

However, the idea of knowledge spillovers between firms and universities seems more natural and is partly behind the idea of the French public policy of competitiveness clusters. In this case, the channel of technological transfers would be double: the education of students endowed with skills which fit well firms' needs on the one hand, and the transmission and the adaptation of scientific research to firms on the other hand.

We test that idea using data from the 'Employment Areas Atlas' published by the French National Institute of Statistics (INSEE) in 1998. We found in the Atlas, for each employment area, the number of students in 1996–7 and the number of R&D and consulting plants in 1997. The quality of our data is not optimal since we have neither time dimension nor precise decomposition of the information (by disciplines or fields of knowledge). Consequently, it is impossible to control for many of the sources of biases as we did before; the best we can do is control for fixed characteristics at industry and département levels.

We work with the year 1997 only and we control for unobserved heterogeneity at the industry and département levels.

The number of students in the employment area seems to be, all other things being equal, positively correlated to firms' productivity. Once fixed characteristics of the firm's industry and département have been taken into account, a 100 per cent increase in the number of local students is correlated with an increase of 0.3 per cent of productivity. However, local R&D activity might be a better proxy for spillovers.[18] Indeed, when we add the variable on R&D, the effect of the number of students disappears. We also observe some spatial and sectoral sorting: firms located in an employment area with a high level of R&D and consulting activities are also firms which belong to highly productive départements and industries. Nevertheless, once we control for this effect, a positive and significant correlation between firms' productivity and local research activity still remains: doubling the number of R&D and consulting plants in the employment area is associated, everything else being equal, with a 2.3 per cent higher TFP.

Our data do not allow us to control for all unobserved heterogeneity and for simultaneity bias; we consequently cannot clearly interpret those results in terms

[18] Note that the two variables are very highly correlated, with a correlation coefficient of 83%.

of causality. However, there is a positive and highly significant correlation between R&D and consulting activities in the employment area and firms' productivity: this provides some support to cluster policies which investigate the relationships between firms and research institutions.

4.5.4 *How are cluster benefits distributed?*

Clustering brings economic benefits in terms of higher productivity. But who benefits from these gains? Consumers, workers, capital owners, and land owners are the usual suspects. If the economy was perfectly competitive and all factors of production perfectly mobile, the productivity gains would come in the form of lower prices to consumers. However, this is not likely to be the case in reality. This is important because if land owners capture a large part of the gains (in the form of higher land prices), this would lower the incentive for workers and firms, who generate those gains, to locate in clusters. Consequently, gains from clusters wealth would not be maximized.

In order to address this question, we replicate the preceding exercise on the average wage and the level of profit per unit of capital at firm level. Our results suggest that the gains we measure for workers and capital owners at firm level are positive: a 1 per cent increase in the number of employees in the other firms of the same 3-digit industry in the employment area generates an increase of 0.024 per cent of the average wage and of

0.046 per cent of the profit per unit of capital. However, they are not statistically significant. Even if they were, these numbers suggest that not all the benefits of clustering go to the two factors of production mentioned. Remember that our estimate of the elasticity for the effect of clustering on TFP is 0.049. Using our estimate of the share of labour (around 80 per cent) and of capital (around 20 per cent) in the production function, this means that what goes to these two factors of production is around: $0.8 \times 0.024 + 0.2 \times 0.046 = 0.028$. Remember that our estimate of the elasticity for the effect of clustering on TFP is 0.049 so only part of this gain goes to labour and capital. Hence, this suggests that another factor of production certainly captures a large part of the benefit from clusters and the prime suspect is land. From a theoretical point of view, indeed, the most immobile factor is the factor that should benefit most from the benefits of clustering. Given that we do not have direct evidence of the effect of clusters on land prices, these results should be taken with caution and we can only say that they are consistent with the view that land will disproportionately benefit from cluster effects. If confirmed, they suggest that those rents could be taxed through higher land taxation (see George 1884 for example).

4.6 Is there insufficient clustering?

One advantage of quantifying (even imperfectly) the gains from clustering is that we can compare the actual economic geography and the one we estimate to be optimal from the point of view of maximizing productivity. At face value, our previous result that productivity increases with clustering would imply (even though the gains are modest) that more clustering is always better. Of course, this cannot be the case because at some point cluster gains may reverse into congestion costs. Those are the questions we address in this section.

4.6.1 Localization vs. congestion effects

We have considered so far that localization economies were linear, e.g. that the productivity of a firm was growing at the same rate, whatever the density of employees of its own sector in its area was. However, besides cluster benefits, congestion effects also exist. These congestion effects could affect the utility of agents (through increased traffic, pollution, etc.) which we cannot measure, but could also impact negatively the productivity of firms. In this case, the productivity–cluster relationship would take the form of a bell curve: productivity would increase at low levels of clustering and would then decrease with clustering. We test that idea by using a non-linear specification. We also reduce the sample to single-plant firms for which congestion effects should be better measured. We graph the relation between total factor productivity gains of firms and our measure of clustering (the number of other employees in the same sector and in the location of the firm in question). As we can see in Figures 4.1 and 4.2, all else being equal, the evolution

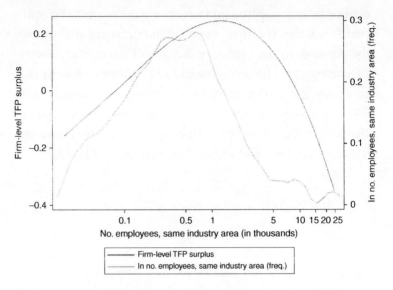

Figure 4.1 Localization economies: employment area/Naf 3-digit

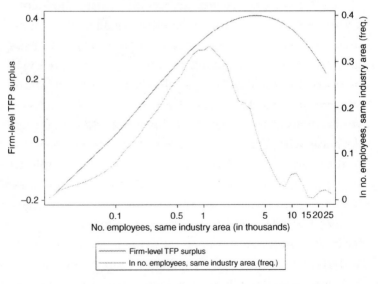

Figure 4.2 Localization economies: département/Naf 3-digit

of productivity at firm level with the thickness of its own industry on its territory has clearly a bell shape, either at the employment area or at the département level. This means that for a firm, the increase in our measure of clustering improves productivity up to a point at which congestion effects dominate. Not surprisingly, the maximum of productivity gains is attained for a bigger number of employees at the département level than at the employment area level: since départements are larger than employment areas, the threshold from which congestion effects dominate cluster economies is higher.

4.6.2 Optimal vs. observed geography

As we have already discussed in Chapter 2 there are many reasons why market forces may not deliver the optimal economic geography. Several market failures can be identified in the spatial dimension and this is one reason why public intervention is both justified and complex. Also, theory does not tell us whether we should expect economic geography to be too concentrated or too dispersed compared to the optimum. Can we answer this question from an empirical point of view? Only up to a point because we cannot measure all welfare implications of economic geography (for consumers for example). Namely, we can answer the following question: is the observed geography too concentrated or too dispersed relative to the economic geography that maximizes productivity? Figures 4.1 and 4.2 allow us to compare the observed distribution of firms (the grey curve) with the estimated curve of productivity gains (the darker curve) as a function of our clustering measure. We first note that the distribution of the cluster variable has the same shape as the curve of estimated gains. There are few firms which choose to locate in places where the number of workers in the same sector is very small. There are also few firms which choose to locate where already 'too' many workers of the same sector work.

This suggests that French firms do internalize in their location choice part of the positive gains of agglomeration and some of the congestion costs. However, both graphs suggest that they have not internalized them completely. Indeed, employment areas and départements seem to be undersized or more exactly underspecialized: the peak of the distribution of firms is attained before the level of sectoral clustering for which productivity gains are maximum. The difference between the peak of the distribution (650 employees) and the peak of the estimated productivity gains (1,270 employees)[19] is sizeable and it suggests consequently that there is scope for public intervention that leads to a more clustered economic geography. However, the potential productivity gain is not very large: if firms at the peak of the distribution reach the estimated peak for productivity gains, everything else being equal, we find that they would increase their productivity by around 2.1 per cent. This productivity gain would be obtained with an

[19] The graph shows the logarithm of the cluster measure on the horizontal axis.

important change in geographic specialization. Also, for some sectors, though a minority, the effect of such a change could be negative for productivity spillovers: our results are only average results for all the manufacturing industries. Moreover, the congestion effects we take into account are congestion effects at firm level; we do not control for the congestion effects for the individuals (pollution, higher land prices, overcrowding for existing transport infrastructures, etc.). The last French census has shown that the Île-de-France region, in spite of its key role in wealth creation for the country, tends to lose people whereas periphery regions, such as the western part of the country, or more generally rural areas, seem to have become more attractive. Explanations in terms of quality of life are often given to explain those evolutions and suggest that the welfare costs of big agglomerations are large for individuals. Besides, such mechanisms were mentioned by Cingano and Schivardi (2004) to explain why empirical studies in the 1990s usually found that local specialization tended to reduce employment growth. Finally, remember that a high level of local specialization carries risks as it means that a negative sectoral shock generates a local recession. Surely, the gap between the observed and the estimated peaks partly reflects some of those costs we cannot control for in our estimation.

What can we conclude at this point? The empirical analysis on firm-level French data shows that economic clusters produce economic gains. The observed distribution of firms suggests that some of these gains are internalized by economic agents in their location choice. Indeed, geography matters for firms: it is clear that a firm that would choose to locate in a region with no other firm of its sector would forfeit large productivity gains: our estimation graphed above indicates that this productivity loss would be around 25 per cent relative to the location at the peak of the observed distribution. Hence, clusters appear as the natural consequence of location choices by firms. From this point of view, at least in the French case, the economic geography brought by market forces does not seem very much under specialized from the point of view of firm total factor productivity. Hence, the logical next question is: can public policies and in particular cluster policies be used to help clusters develop and reap the (modest) gains associated with more clustering? Are cluster policies the best tool to produce these productivity gains? These are the questions we examine in the next chapter through the analysis of a specific cluster policy.

5

Public Support for Clusters: A Case Study on French 'Local Productive Systems'

5.1 Introduction

In 1999, the Délégation Interministérielle à l'Aménagement et à la Compétitivité des Territoires (DIACT, formerly DATAR), the French administration in charge of regional policy, implemented a public policy devoted to promoting relationships between firms located in the same area and belonging to the same industry. The policy consists in subsidizing a group of firms presenting a collective action project. This is clearly a policy inspired by the literature on positive effects of 'clusters' on competitiveness. It is the first public policy in favour of clusters in France, but it is not the first experience in the world. Since the beginning of the 1990s, many countries or regions such as Germany, South Korea, Brazil, or the Spanish Basque country have had public policies supporting clusters. Those policies are very often inspired by the example of Italian industrial districts. Italian industrial firms are indeed characterized by a strong tendency to clustering so that the peninsula is covered by many industrial clusters, often specialized in traditional sectors (leather goods, shoes, furniture, etc.).[1]

We try in this chapter (based on a more technical paper by Martin et al. 2008b) to assess the efficiency of this public policy intended to promote clusters, principally measuring the impact of being in an LPS (local Productive System) on firms' total factor productivity. As far as we know, this chapter is the first econometric attempt to evaluate the effect of a cluster policy. Some case studies exist but we are not aware of any quantitative work. There are however two related questions that have been studied by economists. Cluster policies have two dimensions: one is focused on promoting innovation and performance in chosen industries, and has therefore a very strong industrial policy flavour. On the other side, cluster policies always insist on the importance of the local territory with the underlying idea that technological spillovers are localized. This resembles regional policy motivations. Both industrial and regional policies have attracted empirical economists' attention.

5.2 Does policy affect location? A review

Beason and Weinstein (1996) measure the impact of various industrial policies in Japan between 1955 and

---

[1] Whereas several rich economies, faced with increased competition from developing countries, experienced in the 1980s a decline of their traditional industries, Italy seems to have resisted quite well.

1990. Japan is often presented in case studies as the best example of successful targeted industrial policies (in the semiconductor industry, for example). They show that even though one of the official aims of Japanese industrial policies was to foster the growth of some industrial sectors, there is, on average, a negative correlation between the growth of a given industry and the intensity of the aid it received for all types of instruments (textiles and mining in particular received a large amount of aid but experienced a very slow growth compared to other sectors), which casts doubt on the role of industrial policies and of targeting by public authorities. Besides political economy explanations ('pork-barrel politics'), the authors evoke the desire of authorities 'to offset economic dislocation that might arise due to the collapse of industries' and the attempt 'to raise the productivity in these sectors in order to maintain their competitiveness'. But they later show that industrial policies have had no significant impact on total factor productivity growth (at the industry level). Lawrence and Weinstein (1999) in a study assessing the role of trade in Japanese growth over the period 1964–73 find again no effect of various industrial policy tools on industries' total factor productivity (TFP) growth.

Closer to the subject of this chapter, some authors studied the role of regional policies on location decisions of firms. Crozet et al. (2004) study for example the determinants of location choice by foreign investors in France over the period 1985–95. They find strong evidence of agglomeration patterns in FDI; the probability for a foreign firm to locate in a given area highly increases with the number of other firms of the industry in that area. They measure then the impact of a French subsidy and of European grants for regional policy on firm location choice. They find no significant effect of those policies once fixed location effects are controlled for. Devereux et al. (2007) study the effect of Regional Selective Assistance (RSA) grants[2] on firms' location in the United Kingdom. They find a positive but extremely weak effect of the policy. The interesting point of their study is that the effect of the grant is greater if the potential of localization economies in the area is higher. Consequently, agglomeration effects seem to be of greater importance for firms' location choice than monetary subsidy.

More recently, Criscuolo et al. (2007) study the impact of RSA on firms' employment, investment, and TFP. They use an original strategy of instrumentation in order to control for the usual endogeneity biases that the evaluation of industrial policies suffers from. They find a positive impact of the policy on employment and investment, but not on productivity. In fact, it seems that the programme, by supporting less efficient firms, may slow down reallocation from less efficient plants, which could affect negatively the aggregate productivity growth.

Beyond this, existing policies appear to either attempt to foster the geographical concentration of industries (like most cluster initiatives) or, instead, disperse them (like UK regional assistance grants and most other policies from an earlier vintage in Europe). Policies that

[2] Which are very similar to the French 'Prime d' Aménagement du Territoire' (PAT).

attempt to disperse industries seem to ignore the existence of agglomeration economies and the fact that firms often make their location choice for good reasons. This generates deadweight losses and limits the effects of those policies as shown by Devereux et al. (2007). Cluster policies on the other hand seem to overestimate the benefits from clustering as argued above. As a result, costly policies are undertaken to generate only small benefits in terms of strengthened agglomeration. The other pitfall of these cluster policies is that they fail to recognize that the location decisions of firms are driven by considerations more complex than the specialized cluster vs. dispersion dichotomy.

For instance, a good case can be made that specialization may be beneficial only to firms at particular stages of their life-cycle and only to some of the activities that they conduct. In their review of the evidence, Duranton and Puga (2000) show that local specialization, i.e. clusters, benefits mainly mature firms. Newly created firms appear to benefit more from diverse local environments in which developing new production processes is easier. In a slightly different vein, sectoral specialization appears to profit production activities much more than other activities such as headquarters (Duranton and Puga 2005). Hence attracting new firms to clusters may be more complicated than often envisioned and one-size-fits-all policies towards clustering may not work well.

In our work, we try to assess the effect of a specific policy and assess the capacity of public subsidies to foster externalities, and in doing so productivity, in agglomer-ated areas.[3]

5.3 What are the 'Local Productive Systems'?

5.3.1 *The policy*

The French agency in charge of regional policy (DIACT) issued in 1998 a tender intended to fund collaborative projects between firms of a given industry located in the same area. The purpose was clearly to promote agglom-eration externalities and clusters dynamics. This policy corresponds to a quite radical shift in the objectives of French regional policy, from traditional spatial equity to taking more into account efficiency considerations in geographic distribution of economic activities. One of the motivations was to replicate the alleged success of Italian industrial districts in the 1980s: the idea was to enhance, through public intervention, collaborations which developed 'naturally' in Italy.

A large number of projects were submitted and around fifty of them received a subsidy in 1999. An additional fifty were funded in 2000, when the agency in charge issued a new tender. The tender was then transformed as a permanent one, and each year new or old propositions (only a handful of them now) are getting approved and funded by an ad hoc national commission.

[3] The results presented in this chapter are part of a more technical work by Martin et al. (2008b).

At the beginning, funding criteria were not extremely strict. The announced aim of the policy was to give a small monetary incentive (the mean subsidy more or less equals 37,500 euros) to set off or reinforce clusters. Conditions are now more demanding (established collaborations, credibility of the proposed action, knowledge of direct competitors, etc.). The policy funds a project and not directly a group of firms. Very often, local authorities are the official candidate organizing the project, and firms join once the structure has secured the necessary funding. A wide range of actions can be funded: a study of feasibility for the development of a common brand, the creation of a grouping of employers, or the implementation of collective actions in the field of exports, for instance. The geographical scale of an LPS is generally the département (94 of them on continental France) or the employment area (341 of them).

5.3.2 The data

We use the same French annual business survey[4] data as above, when evaluating agglomeration effects. The information is available at both the firm and plant levels. The data set covers all firms with more than twenty employees in the manufacturing industry and all plants of those firms. Our data cover the period 1996–2004.

At the firm level, we have all accounting data (production, value added, employment, capital, exports,

---

[4] Called in French 'Enquêtes annuelles d'entreprises'.

aggregate wages, etc.) and information about firm location, firm industry classification, and firm structure (number of plants etc.). At the plant level, data are less exhaustive; they principally include location, industry classification, number of employees, and information about the parent firm. The main variables needed, firm's value added, employees, and capital, are directly available (measured at the beginning of the year) in the business annual surveys.

We obtained from the DIACT the list of LPS and information about the subsidies obtained, the structure which holds them, etc. We contacted individually during the year 2006 around 90 LPS, to ask them the names and addresses of member firms. Workable files were obtained for 56 of them, which represents 3,234 firms. Unfortunately, the biggest loss of information comes later, when merging those firms with the annual business surveys. We merge successfully only 641 firms (the others are probably firms with less than 20 employees or with poorly collected information), from 45 LPS.

From a geographic point of view, we dropped all firms located in Corsica and in overseas départements. Consequently, our sample covers the 94 and the 341 continental French départements and employment areas.

More observations are dropped: the ones for which value added, employment, or capital is missing, negative, or null.[5] In the end, the sample is an unbalanced panel

---

[5] We also try to get rid of outliers in our sample, dropping 1% extremes for the following variables: average labour productivity, capital intensity, and capital stock growth rate.

involving 479 firms which belong to an LPS. Eighty-eight 3-digit industrial sectors and thirty-nine LPS are represented.

We are now turning to the question whether those industries and firms concerned by LPS projects are a distinctive group within the French economy.

5.3.3 Are LPS industries different?

The first interesting investigation concerns industries. The traditional operation mode of regional policies in France, but also in other comparable countries, is to try to help industries identified as suffering from structural difficulties. Since industries are usually quite concentrated in a country, the regional dimension of the policy can be justified. Note also that with the recent strengthened restrictions from the EU legislation on state aids, this industry-driven temptation of regional policy becomes even more obvious.

We show in Table 5.1 levels and evolutions of average labour productivity, capital intensity, and export share for three different groups of industries: industries which are not represented in the LPS (25), industries with less than ten LPS firms (46), and industries with at least ten LPS firms (16).

The statistics of Table 5.1 are quite illustrative. In 1996, average labour productivity is lower in industries where LPS are well represented than in the other manufacturing industries. Note that this result is perhaps not so surprising once you notice in the second line that those LPS

Table 5.1 Industry-level summary statistics

Variables	Non-LPS-treated industries	Industries with less than 10 LPS-treated firms	Industries with at least 10 LPS-treated firms
Average level in 1996			
Labour productivity	43.64	43.54	37.64
Capitalistic intensity	65.72	57.27	40.31
Export share	0.34	0.34	0.24
Evolution between 1996 and 2004 (in %)			
Employees	−10.68	−8.82	−3.84
Value added	19.30	23.26	26.27
Labour productivity	34.54	32.54	34.31
Exports	23.19	50.15	56.81

Note: Labour productivity = value added/employees, capitalistic intensity = capital stock/employees, export share = export value/sales. Values are in thousands of real euros.

industries appear to be much more labour intensive than the others. Between 1996 and 2004, the employment loss for the average non-LPS French manufacturing industries is 10.68 per cent. LPS industries lost less employment, considerably less (3.84 per cent) for the industries with the most important LPS implication. Note that the value added of those industries increased more (26.27 per cent and 23.26 per cent vs. 19.30 per cent), but not in a way proportional to employment changes, so that labour productivity increased on average by 34.54 per cent in the non-LPS manufacturing industries, and by only 32.54 per cent and 34.31 per cent in LPS industries.

To summarize, LPS industries are on average much more labour intensive than the rest of manufacturing; they preserved a larger part of their employees in the 1996–2004 period but they also made less important productivity gains.

5.3.4 *Are LPS firms different?*

The summary statistics of firms belonging or not to an LPS are provided in Table 5.2. The firms involved in an LPS are bigger than the others, either in terms of value added or in terms of employees and capital stock. They nevertheless tend to be less productive. It is also interesting to note that they are more homogeneous than the others, since for each variable (except for the number of employees), the standard deviation is larger for non-LPS firms.

Table 5.2 Summary statistics about firms

Variable	LPS firms			Non-LPS firms		
	Obs	Mean	Std. Dev.	Obs	Mean	Std. Dev.
Value added	3227	11717.18	35210.83	167002	6502.27	43465.85
Employees	3227	257.98	718.15	167002	131.52	652.03
Capital stock	3227	16927.36	65984.53	167002	8257.74	106165.30
Labour productivity	3227	39.80	16.57	167002	41.51	19.50

Note: Value added, capital, and labour productivity are expressed in thousands of real euros.

5.3.5 *How are LPS allocated?*

We then try to explore how pre-entry firm-level average characteristics can explain the probability that a firm becomes an LPS firm. The analysis confirms that LPS firms are bigger than the others, and that when compared to the whole set of firms, they tend to be less productive. However, this negative pre-entry productivity differential is mainly explained by the fact that LPS firms belong to declining industries and are located in less productive areas. They also benefit more from public subsidies than the others. One interpretation is that LPS firms are important for local politicians because they are big employers and that they are good at lobbying for public subsidies. Finally, the clusters they belong to are small clusters, which are relevant at the local level but not at the national level.

These results about the determinants of entry into the LPS scheme tend to show that the revealed objectives of the LPS policy are very close to the goals of traditional regional policies.

5.4 Do firms gain from the LPS policy?

We now proceed to estimate the effects of the LPS policy on firms. The natural dependent variable for this estimation is total factor productivity. The aim of the policy is indeed clearly to foster collaborations between firms and to enhance agglomeration externalities, which should translate most notably into higher TFP. We use a measure of TFP at the firm level, obtained through the estimation of production functions at the 2-digit industry level by ordinary least squares (OLS). Hence, we control for employment and capital of the firms.

We first estimate the effect of the LPS policy without controlling for the sector and the départements in which the firm produces.[6] Figure 5.1 presents graphically the time pattern of the LPS effect. The deviation with respect to the horizontal line at zero tells us how an LPS firm performs compared to the non-LPS firms before and after it gets the LPS label: two years before and up to five years after it gets the label. Compared to other firms, LPS firms are not statistically different in terms of TFP two years before they get the label. However, they then perform badly relative to the non-LPS firms and a growing productivity gap between both types of firms appears. The difference is always statistically significant during the years following entry into the LPS scheme (the shaded area around the line is the 5 per cent confidence interval). Does this mean that the LPS label is actually detrimental to firms? One should not jump to this conclusion. Figure 5.2, where we control for the département in which the firm is located, and Figure 5.3, where we also control for the sector firms belong to, explain why. Once the average productivity of the département is controlled for, it appears that before entering in the LPS, firms are rather more productive (even though the

[6] The estimation is a simple OLS with year fixed effects so as to control for the effect of the business cycle.

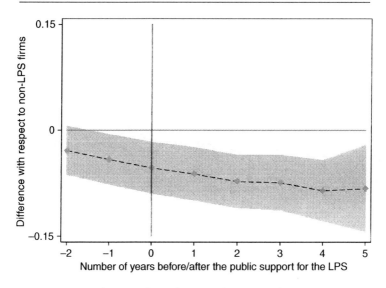

Figure 5.1 LPS firms and productivity/no control

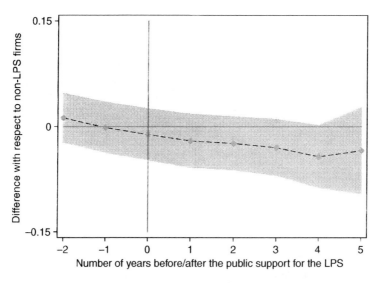

Figure 5.2 LPS firms and productivity/département control

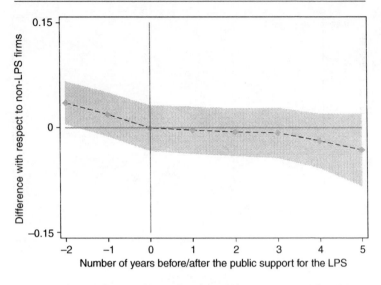

Figure 5.3 LPS firms and productivity/département and industry control

differential is not significant at the 5 per cent level) than the other firms of the département. What it means is that LPS firms are located in départements that are less productive than the others. Moreover, the slope of the curve is still negative but the differential of productivity is not significant any more. Figure 5.3 shows the same estimation when we add a control for the sector. Hence it asks the question: how does the productivity of a firm evolve when it gets the LPS treatment with respect to firms in the same département and in the same sector? We see that LPS firms tend to be significantly more productive than non-LPS firms two years before they get the label. Moreover, they still are on a negative trend but, in this case, the slope of the curve is much less negative

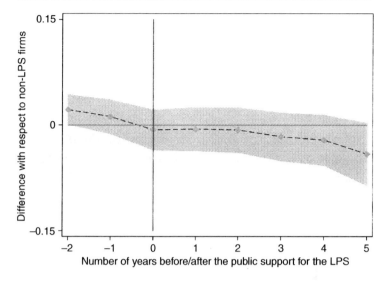

Figure 5.4 LPS firms and productivity/individual control

and post-entry productivity differential is never significant. This suggests that the negative effect of LPS in Figure 5.4 was actually due to a selection effect: firms that obtained the LPS label were in less productive regions and in declining sectors. We also analyse whether the LPS treatment affects the productivity of a firm relative to its own average for the period.[7] Again, no statistically significant effect of the LPS policy can be detected.

5.4.1 *LPS and single-plant firms*

Firms may be affected differently by the LPS policy. In particular small firms or/and single-plant firms may be

[7] Techinically, this means introducing firm fixed effects in the regressions to control for any unobserved variable specific to the firm that could affect its productivity.

153

affected very differently from large, multi-plant or multi-national firms. The latter ones are probably less affected by their local environment than smaller firms. We try to abstract from this potential downward bias of the LPS effect by focusing on single-plant firms. There is also another reason to focus on single-plant firms: our data on value added and therefore on productivity are available at the firm level, not at the plant level. Hence, a plant that belongs to an LPS may see its productivity increase but this may not show up at the firm level. Focusing on single-plant firms eliminates this potential bias. Results are presented in Figures 5.5 to 5.8. These confirm the main benchmark results: LPS firms were selected in less productive regions and in declining

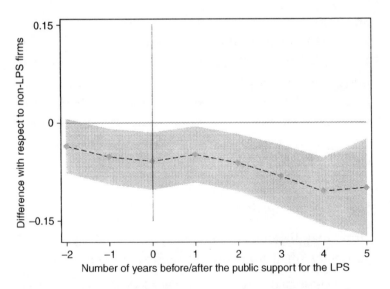

Figure 5.5 LPS single-plant firms and productivity/no control

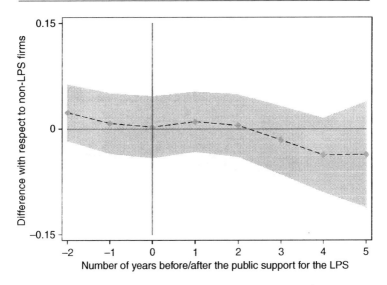

Figure 5.6 LPS single-plant firms and productivity/département control

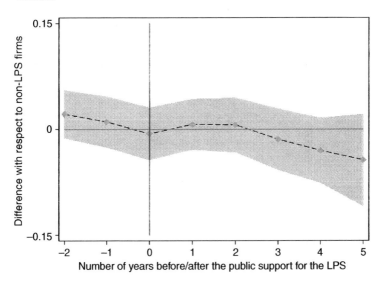

Figure 5.7 LPS single-plant firms and productivity/département and industry control

155

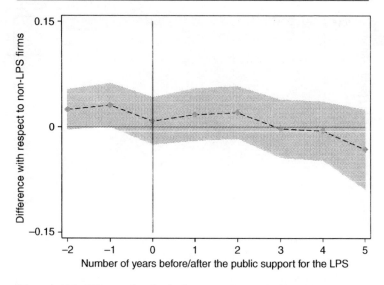

Figure 5.8 LPS single-plant firms and productivity/individual control

sectors. LPS firms become less productive over time in comparison with non-LPS firms, but once we compare in a given département and in a given sector, there is no difference between LPS and non-LPS firms after the policy is implemented. Now, a small positive effect after entry into an LPS appears. However, this improvement is very small, brief, since three years after the entry firms' productivity tends to fall again, and statistically not significant.

Since those results are slightly more optimistic for the policy, we will exclusively focus on single-plant firms in the following subsections, in order to give the effect its maximum chances.

We also controlled for our clustering effect measure as the LPS may have affected productivity through this effect. However, the main results remain unchanged.

5.4.2 Clusters and subsidies: does money matter?

How much does the financial subsidy matter? We saw in subsection 5.3.1 that in the case of LPS policy, the subsidy was not directly given to firms but rather to a structure in charge of the organization of collaborative actions.

The mean and median subsidy are 45,000 and 38,000 euros respectively, with a minimum around 14,500 euros and a maximum of 58,500 euros. These are clearly small amounts. For all firms involved in an LPS, we controlled for the subsidy to see if the amount influenced the effect of the LPS label on productivity. The coefficient is actually negative: LPS plants that receive more money are those that are doing relatively worse in terms of productivity. This however should not be interpreted as a causal relation: it just says that firms in declining regions and sectors received more. Indeed, when we look at this effect of the amount of the subsidy for a given region and sector, the amount of the financing does not matter. Again, this suggests that like many industrial policies that are officially aimed at helping promising firms, the LPS policy was 'captured' by the weakest ones.

5.4.3 *LPS: additional issues*

We also investigated whether small firms reacted differently from large firms to the LPS label. We found no different effect. LPS projects are coordinated by different types of organizational structures (chambers of commerce, producers' association, local authority). The quality of the governance structure may play a significant role in the response to the policy. We therefore measure the evolution of TFP after entry in an LPS according to the nature of the governance structure. We found no such difference result except (but very weakly) a differential positive effect for the LPS label on productivity when it is coordinated by a local authority rather than by a chamber of commerce or a producers' association.

Conclusion

There are no miracles to be expected from cluster policies. While this sober assessment may not be of any surprise to economists, it should serve as a message of caution to policy makers (both on the right and the left) who in Europe have become enthusiasts on cluster policies. This is not to say that economic gains cannot be expected from clusters. In terms of productivity, the French data and the empirical work on other countries show that the starting point of cluster policies is right: gains exist. They are not negligible but not very large either: an increase at best of 5 per cent to 8 per cent of productivity for firms that see the number of jobs in their region and sector double. This type of change in economic geography is not easily attained. Firms already take into account the gains of clusters in their decisions to locate and public policies do not seem to affect much these location decisions. Does this mean that public policies have no role in economic geography and through their effect on economic clusters on productivity? This would be true if the location of firms was such that the market-driven economic geography was optimal. In the case of France, our results suggest the observed economic geography seems underspecialized (clusters are too small) but the productivity gains of increasing the size of clusters from the observed level to their optimal level would be small. Cluster gains do exist and from that point of view the competitiveness cluster policy is certainly a welcome turning point after years during which the main objective of public policies was to avoid spatial concentration. However, they are largely internalized by firms in their location choice and therefore this puts into doubt the rationale of public policies that would attempt to artificially increase the size of clusters. The analysis of an admittedly modest cluster policy in France, the LPS, shows that going from theory to practice is not an easy task. We found practically no effect on firms' productivity, maybe because the policy has not had any effect on employment in the LPS clusters, e.g. it has not made them more attractive. This is consistent with existing empirical studies that conclude that public policies have only a small impact on firms' location decisions. The only positive impact on productivity—though weak and transitory—we find for this policy is on single-plant firms which may indeed be the most isolated and therefore those that have the most to gain from coordination. If this result is confirmed, this raises doubts on the decision to focus the competitiveness cluster policy on large firms. Remember also that the LPS policy is—contrary to the competitiveness cluster policy—a policy that has not been very costly for public finances. Hence, a generous reading of our results would be that a policy that costs little had little effect on the productivity of firms involved. However, our finding of a strong selection effect in LPS policy in the sense that the label was given to firms, sectors, and regions in relative decline shows that the equity considerations in public policies dealing with economic geography have not disappeared. This suggests that the trade-off between equity and efficiency at the spatial level has not been clarified. The stated objectives and the actual implementation of the policy seem contradictory. The stated objective was not very far from a 'picking the winners' strategy. In fact, our results suggest that 'picking the losers' was closer to reality. Our interpretation is not that the policy should have tried to 'pick the winners' but that any such public policy is in danger of being captured. At the least the coherence between the objectives and the implementation would need some strengthening. Given the modesty of the LPS policy we do not want to draw general conclusions for cluster policies in Europe. However, our results do point to risks that are inherent in such policy, for example that such policies may be captured by interests that alter the stated objectives. Such policies—especially if they are conducted as is the case in France in a centralized manner—deny the sectoral heterogeneity in terms of agglomeration gains. There is no simple intuitive classification of sectors that gain more or less from clustering. Hence, it will be difficult for policy makers to choose sectors for which clustering should be fostered. Such policy may actually deny any chance to territories for which the main asset is the low production cost. A usual critique of industrial policies is that they assume that the state has sufficient information on the 'right' sectors. The same critique can be made on cluster policies that need to know sufficiently to choose both the 'right' sectors and the 'right' territories. If cluster polices succeed in specializing entire regions in specific sectors, they may render these regions very vulnerable to sectoral shocks that globalization makes more likely in the future. This is especially the case in Europe where labour mobility is weak.

Our results suggest that French firms internalize gains from clusters as well as costs from congestion in their location choice. Hence, the aim of public policies should not be to increase artificially the size of clusters. For the reasons stated above, we conclude that a centralized cluster policy that gives subsidies to specific firms, in specific territories, and in specific sectors is not the right answer. Other instruments exist which should focus on the reasons why the development of 'natural' clusters is hindered. Public policies can help increase the gains from existing clusters. Public research infrastructures or education policies may certainly help in that matter but are more general than cluster policies. Public policies can also help reduce congestion costs that are a clear brake on the expansion of clusters. The congestion of networks and of public infrastructures, the reduction of quality of life, are well-known examples. Regulations on zoning, regulations that make it difficult to close and open plants, increase the cost for firms to relocate towards clusters. This conclusion is not entirely new: at the local level, transport policies, the provision of local public goods, local zoning regulations, etc. have always been at the core of local authorities' economic policies. This type of public policy is certainly less exciting than the attempt to create a cluster in bio-technologies or a new Silicon Valley, but is more reasonable in view of the knowledge accumulated by economists on the subject.

Do our results on France extend to other countries? We are confident, given that our results confirm what has been found for other industrialized countries with different methodologies, that our broad message can apply to other rich countries. This may not be so for developing countries and emerging markets where the productivity gains of agglomeration may not have been fully exploited given that these countries' level of spatial specialization and density is generally lower than in industrialized countries. The World Development Report (World Bank 2009) entitled *Reshaping Economic Geography* shows that economic agglomeration 'rises rapidly during its transformation from an agrarian to an industrial economy, which generally coincides with its development from low to middle income'. It also argues that many of the economic mechanisms at work in shaping economic geography in industrialized countries are present in developing countries. Whether the gains from clustering are large and under-exploited, and require active policies—in a context of low institutional development—remains an open and important question for developing countries.

References

ARZAGHI M., and DAVIS, J. C. 2005. Spatial mobility and geographic concentration. Working Paper, US Census Bureau.

BALDWIN, R. E., and OKUBO, T. 2006. Heterogeneous firms, agglomeration and economic geography: spatial selection and sorting. *Journal of Economic Geography*, 6(3): 323–46.

——and ROBERT-NICOUD, F. 2007. Entry and asymmetric lobbying: why governments pick losers. *Journal of the European Economic Association*, 5(5): 1064–93.

BATHELT H., MALMBERG, A., and MASKELL, P. 2004. Clusters and knowledge: local buzz, global pipelines and the process of knowledge creation. *Progress in Human Geography*, 28(1): 31–56.

BAUM-SNOW, N. 2007. Did highways cause suburbanization? *Quarterly Journal of Economics*, 122(2): 775–805.

BEASON R., and WEINSTEIN, D. E. 1996. Growth, economies of scale, and targeting in Japan (1955–1990). *Review of Economics and Statistics*, 78(2): 286–95.

BECKER, R., and HENDERSON, J. 2000. Intra-industry specialization and urban development. In J.-M. Huriot and J.-F. Thisse (eds.), *Economics of Cities: Theoretical Perspectives*. Cambridge: Cambridge University Press, 138–66.

BELLEFLAMME, P., PICARD, P., and THISSE, J.-F. 2000. An economic theory of regional clusters. *Journal of Urban Economics*, 48(1): 158–84.

BESLEY, T., 2006. *Principled Agents? The Political Economy of Good Government*. Oxford: Oxford University Press.

BRIANT, A., COMBES, P.-P., and LAFOURCADE, M. 2010. Dots to boxes: do the size and shape of spatial units jeopardize economic geography estimations? *Journal of Urban Economics*, 67(3): 287–302.

BURCHFIELD, M., OVERMAN, H. G., PUGA, D., and TURNER, M. A. 2006. Causes of sprawl: a portrait from space. *Quarterly Journal of Economics*, 121(2): 587–634.

CHARLOT, S., and DURANTON, G. 2004. Communication externalities in cities. *Journal of Urban Economics*, 56(3): 581–613.

CHESHIRE, P. C., and GORDON, I. R. 1998. Territorial competition: some lessons for policy. *Annals of Regional Science*, 32(3): 321–46.

——and SHEPPARD, S. 2002. The welfare economics of land use planning. *Journal of Urban Economics*, 52(2): 242–69.

CICCONE, A., and HALL, R. E. 1996. Productivity and the density of economic activity. *American Economic Review*, 86(1): 54–70.

CINGANO, F., and SCHIVARDI, F. 2004. Identifying the sources of local productivity growth. *Journal of the European Economic Association*, 2: 720–42.

COMBES, P.-P. 2000. Economic structure and local growth: France, 1984–1993. *Journal of Urban Economics*, 47(3): 329–55.

——DURANTON, G., and GOBILLON, L. 2008. Spatial wage disparities: sorting matters! *Journal of Urban Economics*, 63(2): 723–42.

References

Combes, P.-P., Duranton, G., and Overman, H. G. 2005. Agglomeration and the adjustment of the spatial economy. *Papers in Regional Science*, 84(3): 311–49.

Cooke, P. 2001. Regional innovation systems, clusters, and the knowledge economy. *Industrial and Corporate Change*, 10(4): 945–74.

Cortright, J. 2006. Making sense of clusters: regional competitiveness and economic development. Discussion paper, The Brookings Institution Metropolitan Policy Program.

Council on Competitiveness, Monitor Company, and Porter, M. 2001. *Clusters of Innovation*. National Report, Washington, DC.

Criscuolo, C., Martin, R., Overman, H., and Van Reenen, J. 2007. The effect of industrial policy on corporate performance: evidence from panel data. Technical report. Mimeographed, London School of Economics.

Crozet, M., Mayer, T., and Mucchielli, J.-L. 2004. How do firms agglomerate? A study of FDI in France. *Regional Science and Urban Economics*, 34(1): 27–54.

de Blasio, G., and Di Addario, S. 2005. Do workers benefit from industrial agglomeration? *Journal of Regional Science*, 45(4): 797–827.

Department of the Environment, Transport, and the Regions. 2000. *Planning for Clusters: A Research Report*. London: DETR.

Department of Trade and Industry. 2001a. *Business Clusters in the UK: A First Assessment*. London: DETR.

—— 2001b. *Raising UK Productivity: Developing the Evidence Base for Policy*. London: DETR.

Devereux, M. P., Griffith, R., and Simpson, H. 2007. Firm location decisions, regional grants and agglomeration externalities. *Journal of Public Economics*, 91(3–4): 413–35.

DUMAIS, G., ELLISON, G., and GLAESER, E. L. 1997. Geographic concentration as a dynamic process. Working Paper 6270, National Bureau of Economic Research, http://www.nber.org/.

DURANTON, G. 2007. Urban evolutions: the fast, the slow, and the still. *American Economic Review*, 97(1): 197–221.

—— and OVERMAN, H. G. 2005. Testing for localisation using micro-geographic data. *Review of Economic Studies*, 72(4): 1077–106.

—————— 2008. Exploring detail patterns of UK manufacturing location using microgeographic data. *Journal of Regional Science*, 48(1): 213–43.

—— and PUGA, D. 2000. Diversity and specialisation in cities: why, where and when does it matter? *Urban Studies*, 37(3): 533–55.

—————— 2001. Nursery cities: urban diversity, process innovation, and the life cycle of products. *American Economic Review*, 91(5): 1454–77.

—————— 2004. Micro-foundations of urban agglomeration economies. In V. Henderson and J.-F. Thisse, (eds.), *Handbook of Regional and Urban Economics*. Amsterdam: North-Holland, iv, 2063–117.

—————— 2005. From sectoral to functional urban specialisation. *Journal of Urban Economics*, 57(2): 343–70.

ELLISON, G., and GLAESER, E. L. 1997. Geographic concentration in US manufacturing industries: a dartboard approach. *Journal of Political Economy*, 105(5): 889–927.

—————— and KERR, W. 2010. What causes industry agglomeration? Evidence from coagglomeration patterns. *American Economic Review*, 100(3): 1195–213.

References

EUROPEAN COMMISSION. 2003. *Final Report of the Expert Group on Enterprise Clusters and Networks*. Brussels: European Commission.

FELDMAN, M. P., and AUDRETSCH, D. B. 1999. Innovation in cities: science-based diversity, specialization and localized competition. *European Economic Review*, 43(2): 409–29.

FISCHEL, W. A. 2000. Zoning and land use regulations. In B. Boudewijn and G. D. Geest (eds.), *Encyclopedia of Law and Economics*. Cheltenham: Edward Elgar, ii, 403–42.

FLORIDA, R. 2002. *The Rise of the Creative Class: And How It's Transforming Work, Leisure and Everyday Life*. New York: Basic Books.

FUJITA, M., KRUGMAN, P. R., and VENABLES, A. J. 1999. *The Spatial Economy: Cities, Regions, and International Trade*. Cambridge, Mass: MIT Press.

GEORGE, H. 1884. *Progress and Poverty: An Inquiry into Causes of Industrial Depressions, and of Increase of Want with Increase of Wealth. The Remedy*. London: W. Reeves.

GLAESER, E. L. 2005. Reinventing Boston: 1630–2003. *Journal of Economic Geography*, 5(2): 119–53.

—— and KAHN, M. 2001. Decentralized employment and the transformation of the American city. *Brookings-Wharton Papers on Urban Affairs*, 2: 1–47.

—— —— 2004. Sprawl and urban growth. In V. Henderson and J.-F. Thisse (eds.), *Handbook of Regional and Urban Economics*. Amsterdam: North-Holland, iv, 2481–527.

—— KALLAL, H., SCHEINKMAN, J. A., and SCHLEIFER, A. 1992. Growth in cities. *Journal of Political Economy*, 100(6): 1126–52.

—— GYOURKO, J., and SAKS, R. E. 2006. Urban growth and housing supply. *Journal of Economic Geography*, 6(1): 71–89.

GOMEZ-IBANEZ, J. A. 1996. Big-city transit, ridership, deficits, and politics. *Journal of the American Planning Association*, 62(1): 30–50.

GORDON, I. R., and MCCANN, P. 2000. Industrial clusters: complexes, agglomeration and/or social networks? *Urban Studies*, 37(3): 513–32.

GREENSTONE, M. I., and MORETTI, E. 2004. Bidding for industrial plants: does winning a 'million dollar plant' increase welfare? Working Paper, University of California, Berkeley.

GREENWOOD. M. J. 1997. Internal migrations in developed countries. In M. R. Rosenzweig and O. Stark (eds.), *Handbook of Population and Family Economics*. Amsterdam: North-Holland, iB. 647–720.

HENDERSON, J. 1974. The sizes and types of cities. *American Economic Review*, 64(4): 640–56.

HENDERSON, V. 2003. Marshall's scale economies. *Journal of Urban Economics*, 53(1): 1–28.

——KUNCORO, A., and TURNER, M. 1995. Industrial development in cities. *Journal of Political Economy*, 103(5): 1067–90.

HENRY, N., and PINCH, S. 2000. Spatialising knowledge: placing the knowledge community of Motor Sport Valley. *Geoforum*, 31(2): 191–208.

HOLMES, T. J. 1999. Localisation of industry and vertical disintegration. *Review of Economics and Statistics*, 81(2): 314–25.

JAFFE, A., TRAJTENBERG, M., and HENDERSON, R. 1993. Geographic localization of knowledge spillovers as evidenced by patent citations. *Quarterly Journal of Economics*, 108(3): 577–98.

KRUGMAN, P. R. 1991. Increasing returns and economic geography. *Journal of Political Economy*, 99(3): 484–99.

LAWRENCE, R. Z., and WEINSTEIN, D. E. 1999. Trade and growth: import-led or export-led? Evidence from Japan and

Korea. NBER Working Papers 7264, National Bureau of Economic Research, Inc., July.

LESLIE, S. W., and KARGON, R. H. 1996. Selling Silicon Valley: Frederick Terman's model for regional advantage. *Business History Review*, 70(2): 435–82.

LUCAS, R. J. 1988. On the mechanics of economic development. *Journal of Monetary Economics*, 22(1): 3–42.

MARKUSEN, A. R. 1996. Sticky places in slippery space: a typology of industrial districts. *Economic Geography*, 72(2): 294–314.

——2003. Fuzzy concepts, scanty evidence, policy distance: the case for rigor and policy relevance in critical regional studies. *Regional Studies*, 37(6/7): 701–17.

MARSHALL, A. 1890. *Principles of Economics*. London: Macmillan.

MARTIN, P. 1999. Public policies, regional inequalities and growth. *Journal of Public Economics*, 73(1): 85–105.

——MAYER, T., and MAYNERIS, F. 2008a. Spatial concentration and firm-level productivity in France. CEPR Discussion Papers 6858, June.

————2008b. Public support to clusters: a firm level study of French local productive systems. CEPR Discussion Papers 7102, CEPR Discussion Papers, Dec.

MARTIN, R., and SUNLEY, P. 2003. Deconstructing clusters: chaotic concept or policy panacea? *Journal of Economic Geography*, 3(1): 5–35.

MASKELL, P. 2001. Towards a knowledge-based theory of the geographical cluster. *Industrial and Corporate Change*, 10(4): 921–43.

MELITZ, M., and OTTAVIANO, G. 2008. Market size, trade, and productivity. *Review of Economic Studies*, 75(1): 295–316.

MORGAN, K. 1997. The learning region: institutions, innovation and regional renewal. *Regional Studies*, 31(5): 491–503.

OBSTFELD, M., and PERI, G. 1998. Regional non-adjustment and fiscal policy. *Economic Policy*, 13(26): 640–56.

OECD. 2001. *Innovative Clusters: Drivers of National Innovation Systems*. Paris: OECD.

OTTAVIANO, G. I. 2003. Regional policy in the global economy: insights from the New Economic Geography. *Regional Studies*, 37(6–7): 665–73.

PELLENBARG, P. H. 2005. Firm migration in the Netherlands. Mimeographed, University of Groningen.

PORTER, M. 1990. *The Competitive Advantage of Nations*. New York: Free Press.

——1998a. Clusters and competition: new agendas for companies, governments, and institutions. In *On Competition*. Cambridge, Mass.: Harvard Business School Press, 213–304.

——1998b. Clusters and the new economics of competition. *Harvard Business Review*, 76(6): 77–91.

——2000a. Locations clusters and company strategy. In G. L. Clark, M. P. Feldman, and M. S. Gertler (eds.), *The Oxford Handbook of Economic Geography*. New York: Oxford University Press, 253–74.

——2000b. Location, competition, and economic development: local clusters in a global economy. *Economic Development Quarterly*, 14(1): 15–34.

——2003. The economic performance of regions. *Regional Studies*, 37(6–7): 549–78.

PRUD'HOMME, R., KOPP, P., and BOCAREJO, J. 2005. Evaluation Economique de la politique parisienne des transports. *Review transports*, 434/November–December: 346–59.

References

PUGA, D. 2002. European regional policy in light of recent location theories. *Journal of Economic Geography*, 2(4): 372–406.

PYKE, F., BECCATTINI, G., and SENGENBERGER, W. 1990. *Industrial Districts and Inter-Firm Co-operation in Italy*. Geneva: International Institute for Labour Studies.

RAPPAPORT, J. 2007. Moving to nice weather. *Regional Science and Urban Economics*, 37(3): 375–98.

RIGBY, D. L., and ESSLETZBICHLER, J. 2002. Agglomeration economies and productivity differences in US cities. *Journal of Economic Geography*, 2(4): 407–32.

ROMER, P. M. 1986. Increasing returns and long-run growth. *Journal of Political Economy*, 94(5): 1002–37.

ROSENTHAL, S. S., and STRANGE, W. C. 2001. The determinants of agglomeration. *Journal of Urban Economics*, 50(2): 191–229.

————2003. Geography, industrial agglomeration, and agglomeration. *Review of Economics and Statistics*, 85(2): 377–93.

————2004. Evidence on the nature and sources of agglomeration economies. In V. Henderson and J.-F. Thisse (eds.), *Handbook of Regional and Urban Economics* Amsterdam: North-Holland, iv, 2119–71.

————2008. Agglomeration and hours worked. *Review of Economics and Statistics*, 90(1): 105–18.

SAXENIAN, A. 1994. *Regional Advantage: Culture and Competition in Silicon Valley and Route 128*. Cambridge, Mass.: Harvard University Press.

SHEFER, D. 1973. Localization economies in SMAs: a production function analysis. *Journal of Urban Economics*, 13(1): 55–64.

SÖLVELL, O., LINDQVIST, G., and KETELS, C. 2003. *The Cluster Initiative Greenbook.* Gothenburg: Competitiveness Institute (TCI)/Vinnova.

STORPER, M. 1997. *The Regional World: Territorial Development in a Global Economy.* New York: Guilford.

SVEIKAUSKAS, L. A. 1975. The productivity of cities. *Quarterly Journal of Economics,* 89(3): 393–413.

THOMPSON, P. 2006. Patent citations and the geography of knowledge spillovers: evidence from inventor- and examiner-added citations. *Review of Economics and Statistics,* 88(2): 383–9.

TIEBOUT, C. M. 1956. A pure theory or local expenditures. *Journal of Political Economy,* 64(5): 416–24.

VAN DER LINDE, C. 2003. The demography of clusters: findings from the cluster meta-study. In J. Bröcker, D. Dohse, and R. Soltwedel (eds.), *Innovation Clusters and Interregional Competition.* Berlin: Springer Verlag, 130–49.

WILDASIN, D. 2002. *Urban Public Finance.* London: Harwood Academic Publishers.

WORLD BANK. 2009. *Reshaping Economic Geography.* World Development Report.

Index

financial support 11–12
firms
  local productive systems 147–8
  single-plant 153–7
fixed effect 98–9, 109–10, 150, 153
foreign direct investment 139–40
France 10–13, 70
  annual business survey 111–12
  concentration evolution 75–7
  départements 74–5, 92, 112, 121
  economic geography 73–86
  local productive systems 5, 10,
    12, 17–18, 137–63
  Pôles de Compétitivité 6, 10
Freiburg 2

geography 8–9, 27–8, 57–8, 125–6
  economic 37, 73–86
  optimal vs observed 133–6
Germany 137
  Innovative Regional Growth
    Cores 6
  Kompetenznetze 5
Gini coefficient 73–5, 76
  automobile industry 85
  clothing industry 80
  electrical components
    industry 83
  growth rate 77–9
  metal products industry 82
  rubber/tyres industry 84
globalization 58
goods, mobility of 32
Grenoble 2
growth 47–8
  see also productivity growth

Herfindahl index 114
heterogeneity 8, 99, 108–9
high-tech sectors 16, 58, 98, 105

imperfect competition 41
increasing returns 14, 29–30, 31,
  33, 35, 38, 41, 42

industrial districts 7, 138
industrial policy 2–3
inefficiencies 42–3
infrastructure 54
innovation 54, 106
innovative regional growth cores 6
input-output matrices 89–90, 102
Italy 138
  industrial districts 7, 138
  spatial units 100

Japan 138–9

knowledge
  asymmetry of 60
  cutting-edge 55–6
knowledge diffusion 30–1
knowledge spillover 31, 110, 123
  and agglomeration 126–9
Kompetenznetze 5

labour 121
labour immobility 58
labour intensive industries 145–7
labour market 90, 92, 93, 98, 103
  externalities 111, 123
labour mobility 32, 47–51, 58
labour pooling 30, 90, 102, 124–5
land markets 28, 52, 53
land use 53, 54, 63, 64
land value 70–1, 97
learning 30
learning regions 62
lobbying 61
local development 62–72
local government, role of 24
local labor systems 106
local productive systems 5, 10, 12,
  17–18, 137–63
  allocation of 149
  data 143–5
  firms belonging to 147–8
  gains from 149–58
  industries in 145–7

Index

local productive systems (*cont.*)
  policy 142–3
  single-plant firms 153–7
local productivity 101
localization economies 35, 94,
    106, 108, 123–30
  and congestion 131–3
  distance 125–6
  distribution of cluster
    benefits 129–30
  employees 123–5
  impact of 120–3
location choice 133–6, 138–42

market failure 47–50
Marshall, Alfred 126
  Principles 1
matching 29–30
metal products industry 81, 82
metropolitan areas *see* cities
microelectronics 55
migration 39, 49, 58
Minalogic 2
mobility of goods and factors 32
Modifiable Areal Unit Problem
  (MAUP) 75
Motor Valley 7–8
Munich 2

Naf classification 112–13, 115–17
narrow clusters 92
national champions 2
net returns curve 38, 44, 48
new economic geography 37
North American Industry
  Classification 89

opportunism 67

planning 53
Pôles de Compétitivité 6, 10
political economy 59–61
Porter, Michael 4, 88
  competitive diamond 23–6

Production Industries in London 6
production inefficiencies 42–3
production structure 29–33
productivity 54, 97
  benefits 93–102
  local 101
  local productive systems
    149–58
  single-plant firms 153–7
productivity curve 33–6, 44, 48,
    62–4
productivity growth 63, 64–8
productivity spillover 135
proximity 126
pseudo-optimum cluster size 38,
    45
public goods 63, 71, 72, 162
public policies 26

regional policy 2–3
regional selective assistance
  grants 140
regional specialization 138–42
regions 3–4, 5, 11, 14, 16, 17, 27,
    53, 57–8, 62, 88, 93, 104, 126,
    137, 153–4, 157, 160, 161
research and development 128
restrictive policies 65–6
risk 135
rubber/tyres industry 81, 84

sectoral employment growth 105
sharing 29
Silicon Valley 1–2, 4, 7, 36, 56, 103
SiliconFen 2
simultaneity 97, 99, 108, 110,
    119–20
Single European Act 12
single-plant firms 153–7
skills 99
small firms 153–7
software 55
South Korea 137
spatial concentration 91–2

179